A Summer of Cricket

A Summer of Cricket

Tony Lewis
foreword by John Arlott

PELHAM BOOKS

First published in Great Britain by Pelham Books Ltd
52 Bedford Square, London WC1B 3EF
1976

ISBN 7207 0880 X

Set and printed in Great Britain by
Tonbridge Printers Ltd, Tonbridge, Kent,
in Garamond twelve on thirteen point,
on paper supplied by P. F. Bingham Ltd,
and bound by James Burn, at Esher, Surrey.

Contents

Illustrations

All the photographs in this book have been taken by Patrick Eagar.

Foreword by John Arlott

No one who watched it will ever forget the English cricket season of 1975. Quite phenomenal summer weather framed all but a day or so of constant event. Fifteen Prudential 'World Cup' matches; four Tests between England and Australia; the finals of the Benson & Hedges and Gillette Cups; and six counties in close contention in the County Championship almost to the end – provided the most intensive cricket calendar anyone has ever known.

Those who reported the main matches of that season, apart from simultaneous matches in the Prudential Trophy – and even then, some still contrived to cock an occasional eye at television of another match – must count themselves extremely fortunate to have done so for a living.

This was Tony Lewis's first season as a senior cricket correspondent. Everyone knew him as a talented performer, astute thinker and experienced observer of the game. Within days he had demonstrated his capacity to write perceptively, revealingly, authoritatively and often amusingly, never allowing technical matters to crowd out humour nor tactical judgements to lose touch with humanity.

It was splendid that he established himself so quickly because he is delightful company in the press box or at the bar or table – when he is not writing a book. Often during the season he hammered away at his writing with, as it seemed, a somewhat envious sideways look at others at their leisure. Now he must feel the effort worth while.

He has set down his account of the season as he saw it. He probably was wise not to attempt to include such of the County Championship as he saw. No correspondent could pay adequate attention to that absorbing competition once the Prudential Trophy matches began in June and the Tests followed one another so closely through July and August.

This is the book of an unblinkered cricketer, recalling the words of C. L. R. James 'What do they know of cricket who only cricket know?' It is interesting reading because it was written by an interested man; he watches and reports cricket with as much zest as he played it; makes fair and rounded judgements; and is rarely at a loss for a story to illustrate a point or reveal a person.

It is happy, at a time when a generation of distinguished cricket writers have retired or are about to do so, that the game has acquired another as informed and readable as Tony Lewis. No one, it is said, ever reads a foreword; and it should be pointed out that those who have lingered here would otherwise, by now, be well into his first book.

Introduction

This book attempts to record the high points of the tremendous cricketing summer we witnessed during 1975. It is written as a series of essays, and each one was written at the time of the match or event which it records. We have tried as much as possible to keep the events in chronological order to show how the summer developed.

As you read this book I hope that you will re-live and enjoy what was really a wonderful summer of cricket.

1 The Prospect

I have always thought that you get most out of watching cricket by not expecting too much from a match. Sit patiently at the boundary, immerse yourself in the struggle, nod at the good ball, curse the full toss, but most important of all, recognise the moments of excellence when they arrive. They are uplifting, and cannot be forced. Out of the day-long pattern of cricket comes the brilliant and the banal in their turn, and like a fine game of chess they should not be contrived before their time.

I therefore viewed the summer of 1975 with suspicion, even quiet cynicism. A 'World' Cup was at hand; cricketers from eight countries flown into England, rushed on to various pitches, to smite seven shades of hell out of each others' bowling in one-day 60-over contests—it was too much of a circus act. Indeed, the whole competition would be all over in a fortnight. Where did that leave the lovers of the patient vigil like me?

Furthermore, it could not be a true World competition without South Africa, one of the most talented cricket nations. Not since objections to their racial policy of apartheid had undermined their cricketing contacts, for reasons of disapproval or impracticability, had they played international cricket. That was last in 1969–70 when the Australians toured.

Yet the cricket purists have had to bow their heads to economic necessity. Commercial sponsorship, not gate money, has preserved first-class cricket in England and the Prudential Assurance Company were the organisation brave enough to bite at the idea of this fortnight's jamboree. Immediately they requested the media to refer to it as The Prudential Cup, not the World Cup; perfectly fair under the terms of sponsorship and especially as the latter was a misnomer. Yet, in the minds and mouths of everyone, this was the first ever 'World Cup' and that above every other prospect made cricket in 1975 a unique experience.

The Australians were to compete and it occurred to the administration of the Test and County Cricket Board that the chance should not be lost of pitching those eternal rivals into a shortened Test series with England. They had virtually torn England apart in a six match series during the winter, winning by four Tests to one, but there was more in their attraction beside the Ashes. England had been terrorised, no less, by Dennis Lillee and Jeff Thomson, two genuinely fast bowlers who had extracted frightening bounce and pace out of Australian wickets.

This small, select breed, usually lethal when hunting in pairs like Wes Hall and Charlie Griffith, Frank Tyson and Fred Trueman or Brian Statham, Ray Lindwall and Keith Miller, offer some of the rare sights in cricket. Apart from their runs-up to the wicket, their actions which have to be balanced if they are to last, and all the malice which goes to make world-class fast bowling, there was also the prospect of seeing batsmen mustering their last drain of courage to fight them off.

Wesley Hall, back in 1963, when he was a little too fast for any batsman's comfort, bowled out Glamorgan's opener with the third ball of the day. I put on my gloves, picked up my bat and just before leaving the dressing room for the middle glanced around, I suppose, for a gesture of encouragement from one of the senior players, himself a fine player of the 'quicks'. He was due in after me, and there he was wrapping his false teeth in a handkerchief and sneaking them into his blazer pocket! Yes, every batsman would be all alone when his turn came to step out to face those famous Australian undertakers, Messrs Lillee and Thomson, and it was going to be a rare spectacle for every lover of the game.

What else was there to look forward to? The Australians would tour around many counties, although it must be the first time in their history that Yorkshire have been omitted. The County Championship would go on, the bread and butter of professional cricket in England if you like, fought out over twenty matches for each county, three days to a match.

Then the sponsored one-day spectaculars, all linked with television coverage—the Benson & Hedges Cup Competition in the first half of the season, the Gillette Cup Competition in the second, and Sunday after Sunday from April until September, the John Player Sunday League, the short game played over forty overs a side. It was estimated that first-class cricket in 1975 would cost £2 million. Without the sponsors it would perish.

Thus one-day cricket is devised to bring about instant thrills, big hits for those who often cannot comprehend the delicacies of defence, or the vagaries of wickets covered or uncovered, which shape techniques and make the most adaptable players the best. The maiden over bowled short of a length to a defensive field earns applause all round; the bowler who attacks the batsmen by bowling a fuller length to encourage shots and therefore mistakes, and places slip fielders for that very reason, finds his art unwanted in the brave new sponsored world. Bishen Bedi, India's master of slow, flighted spin, sits on the sidelines every Sunday for his county Northamptonshire.

Did not Alec Bedser, Chairman of the England Selectors, declare in a lighthearted way in a small village hall at Lower Hutt up the superb estuary from Wellington in New Zealand, that he did not believe one-day cricket produced the sort of cricketers England required in Test matches. With a pitcher and a striker and most others scattered around, he saw it more like baseball than cricket.

So whereas the media duly banged the drums of welcome to the eight countries who arrived to compete for this unique Prudential Cup, there were still many lined up with me, who felt that apart from true British rain which could turn everything to farce, the whole contest was just a glossy overture to the four Test matches against Australia; high ideals expressed in the most flimsy romantic form, which would just whet the appetite for the million classical variations on the Aussie-Pommie things to follow.

One unprecedented meeting at Lord's on Friday, June 6th told me that I had been a little hasty with my prejudices.

2 *Royal Overture*

Briefly, at Buckingham Palace, Her Majesty the Queen, with Prince Philip, Prince Charles and Sir Alec Douglas Home, welcomed those who were to play a part in this first ever World Cup. There was a massive 'team' photograph before the players and officials moved on to Lord's. Prince Philip was again there to greet them.

It is easy to be uplifted by the sheer romance of an occasion which brings together cricket teams of eight nations in the presence of His Royal Highness the Duke of Edinburgh, President of the MCC, in the famous Long Room at Lord's.

And why not? It has never happened before that the very best players from Australia, India, East Africa, New Zealand, Sri Lanka, West Indies, Pakistan and England have congregated under one roof in the company of the members of the MCC Committee, county secretaries and their Presidents, as well as a few former Test players.

There was, back in 1912, a Triangular Tournament held in England, when England, South Africa and Australia played nine Test matches. Yet it was the failure of this ambitious undertaking which ensured that no one attempted to repeat it. Let me just quote Wisden.

'The fates fought against the Triangular Tournament. Such a combination of adverse conditions could hardly have been imagined. To begin with, the Australians, who had been allowed to have everything their own way in choosing the time for the first trial of Sir Abe Bailey's ambitious scheme, quarrelled so bitterly among themselves that half

15

their best players were left at home. In the second place, the South Africans, so far from improving, fell a good way below their form of 1907 and, to crown everything, we had one of the most appalling summers ever known even in England. The result is that the experiment is not likely to be repeated for many years to come—perhaps not in this generation.'

Yet from the moment Prince Philip offered his welcome with typical good humour, everyone instinctively realised that this tournament could succeed handsomely if the fine weather held, and if the players honestly accepted the challenge. Their immediate response was encouraging.

Ian Chappell, Australia's captain, assured that his side would fight all the way to win the Cup even though their emotions were pinned more firmly to the retention of the Ashes later in the season. Majid Khan held no doubts that Pakistan, playing under the captaincy of Asif Iqbal this time, were looking forward to doing well. The two minor cricketing countries, East Africa and Sri Lanka, were obviously quiet and guarded. To them it was a moment of pride to be rubbing shoulders with the major Test-playing countries and, for the next fortnight, enjoying equal status. I thought of the lovely old lady who is the groundsman, or rather the groundswoman, at Colombo in Sri Lanka. For years she has tended that square; poured on the early-morning water to persuade the baked earth to give a little, and then tugged the roller by a dirty fraying rope for hours into the heat of the morning. Good pitches make good players, and because of that the Sri Lankans will surely achieve full membership of the International Cricket Conference very soon. Yes, the old lady would give a nod of approval to see her 'boys', champagne cocktails in their hands, lording it with the best in the world.

The quality of the East Africans was rather more uncertain. Many people have given endless service to the game in Kenya, Uganda, Tanzania and Zambia though

Fernando of Sri Lanka scored 98 not out against New Zealand

Return of the Snow-man

New Zealand in casual mood at Lord's. Standing: *D. R. O'Sullivan; B. J. McKechnie; R. J. Hadlee; H. J. Howarth; B. L. Cairns; B. G. Hadlee; G. P. Howarth.* Seated: *R. O. Collinge; B. F. Hastings; G. M. Turner; D. R. Hadlee; K. J. Wadsworth; J. M. Parker*

(facing page) *The day at the Oval when everything Dennis Lillee hurled down arrived in the middle of Alvin Kallicharran's magic bat*

Extrovert head gear and brilliant strokes to match from Majid Khan for Pakistan against Australia at Headingley

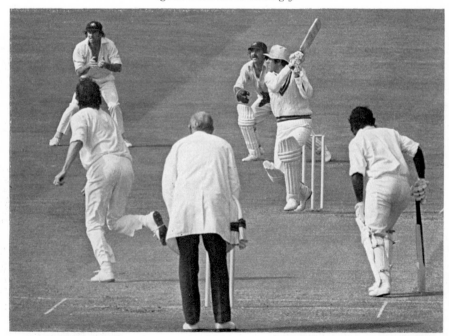

'Cricket lovely cricket' as West Indies tear Australia apart in the Prudential match at the Oval

The all-embracing arms of the law! The game is up for the Lord's streaker

sadly contact with MCC, in a playing sense, was broken in 1970. In fact I was to lead an MCC touring party to East Africa and then on to the Far East but, because MCC had sought to fulfil their traditional commitments with South Africa, political forces leapt at the throats of those who believed sporting contact with a country practising apartheid was beneficial to all. The East Africans refused to entertain MCC and we set off for the Far East instead.

So both these junior teams asked eager questions about limited-over cricket. 'Do we bowl to one side of the stumps to six fielders on that side? Or do we try to bowl straight, wicket to wicket, with five fielders on one side and four on the other? Can we bowl our leg spinner? Would you bowl him early or late?'

Most of the other players had played Tests against each other. Incidentally, Test match cricketers usually have to be dragged to official receptions, like bulls to the market, by the ring through the nose. Yet, for example, even England's Geoff Arnold, who never responds kindly to the chore of sipping cocktails and talking trivia, was seen to be enjoying himself. No one, however hardened to such occasions, ever lost the feeling that he was in on something new. It was a whirl of perpetual surprises. There was New Zealand's Brian Hastings discussing the runners and riders on the English turf with Lance Gibbs of West Indies, with Sunil Gavaskar looking on! Abid Ali, beaming widely, sporting a new beard, eyes shining with the anticipation of returning to green English wickets where the ball moves off the seam for the medium-paced bowlers. Not much joy for him in India. That was it; everyone popped up out of context. Exhilarating, exciting and, most important for my doubting mind, the sight of old enemies sharpened their taste for the battles renewed.

The Australians are very much cocks of the walk with the Ashes in their pockets. Their reputation is perhaps as a tough race, unprepared to suffer fools, and sharp to spit out the criticisms. From a distance this is very much the reputation of Ian Chappell's side, shouting and swearing on the field and unpredictable manners off it. It was their arrival at Lord's on that sunny morning which provided the greatest contrast to the demure 'establishment' look of those awaiting the arrival of the Prince at the rear of the pavilion. The Aussies sauntered through the congregation; casually clothed; trousers flared at the bottom, ties worn with the comfort of dogs with new collars, and most of them sporting hair on the face in the shape of droopy moustaches or balaclava sideburns. Anyone who has read the remarkable verse of Andrew Barton 'Banjo' Paterson, the symbol of the outback for most Australians, might have compared the city-suited MCC representation and the touring Australians, with Banjo's view of the polo match between the infamous up-country, hard-arsed, Geebung Polo Club, and the city smoothies of 'The Cuff and Collar Club'. He wrote of the Geebung players:

> 'And they played on mountain ponies which were muscular and strong,
> Their coats were quite unpolished, and their manes and tails were long,
> And they used to train those ponies wheeling cattle in the scrub
> They were demons were the members of the Geebung Polo Club.'

And I suppose the Aussies could glance around and amuse themselves at the conservative dress of those who flanked their approach to the Long Room, yellow and orange Club ties—men at home in their egg and tomato world. Every bit like the Cuff and Collar Club:

> 'As a social institution 'twas a marvellous success,
> For the members were distinguished by exclusiveness and dress.'

However the Australians dressed or walked, and

perhaps it was simply that we were viewing with
jaundiced eye the living devils who had scourged our
lads in the winter Test series, they very quickly emerged
as a team willing to attack the Prudential competition
and win the Cup.

It is a Cup and prize money well worth winning too.
£9,000 will be divided up between the teams. The
winners to receive £4,000, the losing finalists £2,000,
and the losing semi-finalists £1,000 each. On top of this
there are to be 'Man of the Match' awards—£50 for
each of the first-round matches (£600), £100 for each
semi-final, and £200 for the hero of the final. The
entrants are divided into two groups.

Group A	Group B
England	Australia
East Africa	Pakistan
New Zealand	West Indies
India	Sri Lanka

Every team in a group will play each other once and
the first two teams in each group will go forward to the
semi-finals. The final is to be at Lord's on June 21st.

The matches will consist of one innings per side, each
of 60 six-ball overs and are intended to be completed
in a day, although three days are allocated in case of bad
weather. No bowler is allowed more than twelve overs
and to defeat intimidatory or negative bowling a wide
(one run) will be called if any short-pitched delivery
passes over the head of the batsman standing normally
at the crease, or if the ball does not give the batsman a
chance of playing a stroke.

Each country's side is composed of a squad of 14
players, which means that England cannot dig any more
deeply than that into the resources of the seventeen
counties.

Prudential's magnificent sponsorship which goes into
the game of cricket is £100,000, and of the profits from
the series ten per cent goes to the United Kingdom, 7½

per cent to the remaining teams, and the balance to the International Cricket Conference.

Yet rules, regulations, and cash prizes apart, there was probably more to be gained from the honour of emerging top o' the world. It is a cricket adventure, irresistible to all who are going to watch and play.

As I say, it is too simple to make romantic conclusions about the unifying powers of a simple cocktail party—all nations at peace under one roof. Yet South Africa was absent. How their presence would have adorned the occasion. In cricketing terms, pure and simple, something was missing—you can make a Christmas pudding without brandy, but it is the final ingredient which sets it all alight. Yet this was important and when even the Australians, who were on a major tour, draw their feet up with a beer in hand, in the homes of friends, they will recall with a smile the few moments when all Test teams came together to make one, relished the intercourse, and took the first scent of war to their nostrils.

As we drifted out of Lord's in the early afternoon, there were many people on the patio of the Tavern pub, sipping long cool beers under sunshades, whetting the appetite for the first round battle between England and India on the morrow. An unbroken spell of dry sunny weather increased the optimism. Everything was perfectly set and, even by Olympic standards, nothing could be bettered, save only the bearing of the Prudential torch from Lord's to the other grounds, Headingley, Old Trafford, the Oval and Edgbaston. There was that Olympic feeling, yet it was quickly to be disturbed by an incredible quirk of Indian temperament.

3 The First Round

LORD'S; Saturday, June 7th, 1975

Group A: England beat India by 202 runs

ENGLAND

J. A. Jameson	c Venkat, b Amarnath	21
D. L. Amiss	b Madan Lal	137
K. W. R. Fletcher	b Abid Ali	68
A. W. Greig	lbw Abid Ali	4
M. H. Denness	not out	37
C. M. Old	not out	51
Extras (lb 12, w 2, nb 2)		16
	Total (4 wkts)	334

Innings closed.
Did not bat: B. Wood, A. P. E. Knott, J. A. Snow, P. Lever, G. G. Arnold.
Fall of wickets: 1-54, 2-230, 3-237, 4-245.
Bowling: Madan Lal 12-1-64-1, Ghavri 11-1-83-0, Amarnath 12-2-60-1, Venkat 12-0-41-0, Abid Ali 12-0-58-2, Solkar 1-0-12-0.

INDIA

S. M. Gavaskar	not out	36
E. D. Solkar	c Lever, b Arnold	8
A. D. Gaekwad	c Knott, b Lever	22
G. Viswanath	c Fletcher, b Old	37
B. P. Patel	not out	16
Extras (lb 3, w 1, nb 9)		13
	Total (3 wkts)	132

Innings closed.
Did not bat: M. Amarnath, F. M. Engineer, S. Abid Ali, Madan Lal, S. Venkataraghavan, K. Ghavri.
Fall of wickets: 1-21, 2-50, 3-108.
Bowling: Snow 12-2-24-0, Arnold 10-2-20-1, Old 12-4-26-1, Lever 10-0-16-1, Greig 9-1-26-0, Wood 5-2-4-0, Jameson 2-1-3-0.
England won by 202 runs.
Umpires: D. J. Constant, J. G. Langridge.
Man of the Match: D. L. Amiss.
Adjudicator: J. D. Robertson.

This was the day when India, in front of 16,274 spectators, many of them their devoted fans who had paid
£19,000 to see cricketing history made, committed an
act of senseless perversity. The fanfares heralding a feast
of run-chasing had scarcely died away before they were
refusing even to limp after England's massive target.
England plundered 334 runs for the loss of four wickets,
the highest total ever reached in one-day cricket, and
India refused to try to get them. Was this not rejecting
the whole Prudential idea? Why did they accept the
sponsor's invitation if they did not mean to honour it?
Their reply was 132 for 3 wickets, Sunil Gavaskar batting
through the 60 overs for 36 runs.

Their supporters were desperately disappointed. Many
ran on to the field to plead with Gavaskar and Gaekwad
during the last hour's play. One of them, naked to the
waist, and bearing a flag on a lengthy pole, approached
with the menace of Geronimo. His mission was obviously
peaceful enough. He just wanted to salvage a little pride
in his country by seeing the batsmen go down trying.
During the last half hour anger was borne from the
frustration. There was an unhappy sequence that had
police heavy-footing over the wicket itself in pursuit of
protesters, sights familiar in far off Calcutta or Kanpur
where students are persuaded to light bonfires and even
set fire to stands if boredom or fury descend upon them.
If stands or screens went up in flames at Lord's, at least
it was reasonable to assume the protection of the Pru'
was at hand!

India can also be the most exotic country in which to
play, with the majority as generous as the minority are
undisciplined. K. N. Prabhu, one of their finest writers,
once confessed on his countrymen's behalf, 'You must
expect the unexpected response in a country whose
cricket has drawn a froth of ecstasy and scorn in succeed-
ing breaths; where the silken raiment of success and
sack-cloth hang side by side in the dressing room lockers.'

Yet Indians have never successfully competed at the one-day game in England. Their spin bowlers who serve them so skilfully at home, find the switch from attacking to defensive bowling impossible to master. This time they have left Chandrashekar and Prasanna behind. Venkataraghavan is their captain. His off-spinners are quicker than most and of low trajectory if he wishes to bowl that way. Bishen Bedi is here too, but left out of the side in favour of the seam attack of Abid Ali, Madan Lal, Ghavri, Amarnath and Solkar.

Their mental approach to the game is almost borne out of the heat of the sub-continent, cat-like but un-hurried. Personal politics also permeate the sporting instincts. Did Gavaskar play an innings of demonstration against the omission of Bedi, against the captaincy of Venkat or against the evening meal allowance? His motives could be anything, but after the match the team manager, G. S. Ramchand, made the following statement to the press: 'This is not the way Gavaskar should have played it, and I do not personally agree with his tactics. But he felt that against such a big England total he would get in some batting practice on a good wicket against a good attack. He was told that he should score faster. It's a great disappointment to us but he will not be disciplined.'

Even more disappointing than the spectacle of deadly boring defensive play was the realisation that either India did not wish to progress any further in the competition or they did not understand the rules which read: 'If there are equal points when deciding the semi-finalists, the winner will be the side having won the most matches or, if still equal, the side with the faster scoring rate.' So even if they saw a win over England an impossibility, they could still have done themselves a margin of good in the competition as a whole, should they succeed in other group matches.

Lord's itself was perfection when Dennis Amiss and

John Jameson walked to the middle: sunshine, shirt-sleeves, sahris billowing in gentle breezes. There were sunbathers oblivious to all, and beer drinkers who attacked their pleasure with such verve that they were merry and elated to behold Dennis Amiss's marvellous century, but, soon, they too were oblivious, which was just as well because by then Gavaskar was grinding out his slow pleasure.

What can one say of Amiss other than he stroked a brilliant century on a perfect pitch. It was an innings of calm simple movements. He leaned easily in to his drives, firm-footed, sending the ball speeding over a fast outfield with strong wrists.

His square cutting, executed with a full but chopping swing of the bat, made nonsense of the field placings. I suppose he gracefully cudgelled it, if that is a permissible description. The statistics tell how the assault gathered. Amiss's first 50 came in the 22nd over and his century in the 37th. After Fletcher had assisted with a composed half century, Denness and Old ran amok. With sixes and scrambled singles they scored 89 off the last ten overs in spectacular fashion. In fact 63 runs came off the last five. It was total destruction.

The England bowlers thundered in, over after over, clinically restricting with defensive fields. Snow looked eager on his return to the international field though now, of course, his pace is short of what it was. The fielding was sharp, brimming with concentration.

So India, sadly, presented few problems, though all their bowlers tried desperately hard. If the batsmen had done the same, they would have lost the match but won many friends. The whole idea behind this competition is to strain eye and nerve for victory within the day's play. 'Indian stodge follows England's spice' was the *Sunday Telegraph*'s headline. Across the page the writing was 'Pakistan destroyed by the Sons of Thunder' and that was the match which launched the Prudential Cup high into the skies.

HEADINGLEY; Saturday, June 7th, 1975

Group B: Australia beat Pakistan by 73 runs

AUSTRALIA

A. Turner	c Mushtaq, b Asif Iqbal	46
R. B. McCosker	c Wasim Bari, b Malik	25
I. M. Chappell	c Wasim Raja, b Sarfraz	28
G. S. Chappell	c Asif Iqbal, b Imran	45
K. D. Walters	c Sarfraz, b Malik	2
R. Edwards	not out	80
R. W. Marsh	c Wasim Bari, b Imran	1
M. H. N. Walker	b Asif Masood	18
J. R. Thomson	not out	20
Extras (lb 7, nb 6)		13
	Total (7 wkts)	278

Innings closed.
Did not bat: A. A. Mallett, D. K. Lillee.
Fall of wickets: 1-63, 2-99, 3-110, 4-124, 5-184, 6-195, 7-243.
Bowling: Malik 12-2-37-2, Asif Masood 12-0-50-1, Sarfraz Nawaz 12-0-63-1, Asif Iqbal 12-0-58-1, Imran Khan 10-0-44-2, Wasim Raja 2-0-13-0.

PAKISTAN

Sadiq Mohammad	b Lillee	4
Majid Khan	c Marsh, b Mallett	65
Zaheer Abbas	c Turner, b Thomson	8
Mushtaq Mohammad	c G. Chappell, b Walters	8
Asif Iqbal	b Lillee	53
Wasim Raja	c Thomson, b Walker	31
Imran Khan	c Turner, b Walker	9
Sarfraz Nawaz	c Marsh, b Lillee	0
Wasim Bari	c Marsh, b Lillee	2
Asif Masood	c Walker, b Lillee	6
Naseer Malik	not out	0
Extras (lb 4, w 3, nb 12)		19
	Total	205

Overs: 53.
Fall of wickets: 1-15, 2-27, 3-68, 4-104, 5-181, 6-189, 7-189, 8-195, 9-203.
Bowling: Lillee 12-2-34-5, Thomson 8-2-25-1, Mallett 12-1-49-1, Walters 6-0-29-1, Walker 12-3-32-2, G. S. Chappell 3-0-17-0.
Australia won by 73 runs.
Umpires: T. W. Spencer, W. E. Alley.

Man of the Match: D. K. Lillee.
Adjudicator: R. Appleyard.

The gates were closed soon after the start with about 21,000 spectators in the ground. The cricket was hard and fluctuating. Whoever would have dreamed that one day Australia and Pakistan would be answering a cricket challenge on a ground in Yorkshire?

Perhaps it is more logical to think of Pakistan playing there because Leeds, Bradford and the environs house a large expatriate Pakistani population. It was almost a 'home' match, and the presence of the hordes waving green and white flags and shouting 'gelde, gelde' (faster, faster) as their heroes sped up and down the wicket, gave the day a colour and an intensity which few could have anticipated.

No one could have guessed that the Aussies, who still shout out their preferences for a longer game than 60 overs, would have handled Pakistan so skilfully. Mind you, brave horses may not fancy the fences looming ahead, but they never shy away. Once Ian Chappell's side had voiced its prejudices, it digested the battle orders.

Pakistan were favourites to win this match. Apart from the vocal chorus which made them as comfortable at Headingley as they might have been in Hyderabad, they had players who were much more accustomed to the variety of English wickets; the tendency for the ball to keep low, to move laterally off the seam and to swing longer than usual with the new ball. This was nothing new to Sadiq (Gloucestershire), Majid (Glamorgan), Zaheer (Gloucestershire), Mushtaq (Northants), Asif Iqbal (Kent), Imran (Worcestershire) and Safraz (Northants). Only one Australian, Greg Chappell, who played a couple of seasons for Somerset six years ago compared in experience, though, of course, the few of them who toured in 1972 will have vivid recollections of a Test defeat suffered on a strange turning wicket on this same

Headingley square. A fungus known generally as fuserium disease afflicted the pitch and, let it suffice to say that, the ball was made to perform unexpected tricks by Derek Underwood.

Pakistan beat England in the Prudential matches last season so their talents in the short game, and their understanding of it, are as formidable as anyone's.

Yet into the psychological scales had to be dropped the experience of Pakistan in Australia back in the winter of 1972–73 when they were thoroughly routed, so much so that their captain, Intikhab Alam, was told mid-series that he had lost the job for the next one. Majid then took over against MCC, that was in March 1973. When Pakistan returned to England for a three match series in the summer of 1974 Intikhab had been reinstated. Come the Prudential World Cup, Intikhab had gone again, not only from the seat of captaincy, but out of court altogether. His leg-spin bowling was probably thought a luxury they could not carry in limited-over cricket, but whatever the reasons (and one can never be absolutely certain about the Board of Control for Pakistan, who often move in a mysterious way), this time a completely new captain was chosen in Asif Iqbal.

Add to all this two of the finest fast bowlers in the world, Dennis Lillee and Jeff Thomson, and it is easy to see how the Prudential idea was given wings by this match in the North.

The wicket had no spite. Australia took first use of it and made steady advance. The left-handed Alan Turner found much of the bowling directed at his legs, and like all Australians needed no firmer invitation than that to clip the ball hard through mid-wicket. His New South Wales colleague, Rickard McCosker appeared to slumber but between them they advanced the cause to 30 in the first 10 overs, and then doubled that in the next five. That was the springboard, but fine bowling by Asif Masood, Safraz, and Malik had many playing and missing, and led Pakistan to the verge of a major break-through. Turner's vigorous innings had ensured a run-rate of four an over, but safe catching by a most athletic collection of fielders reduced Australia to 124 for 4. At this moment Greg Chappell was battling to find the middle of his bat. He let loose one or two thumping straight drives, but edged the ball just as often. If Asif could just trap one more wicket now, either Edwards or Chappell, then at least he would only have to contend with wicket-keeper Rod Marsh and the bowlers. No one would underestimate Marsh's batting, but he was less likely to build up the innings that mattered than the two front-liners.

This was a prototype Edwards situation. His job was, as it had been so many times in his Test career, to reupholster his country's innings. He shuffled nervously around the crease and survived a loud appeal for lbw when he was 7 facing up to Asif Masood. Australia looked down in the world, and declined further when Greg Chappell tried to hit Imran over the top and was caught at cover. From a distance this looked an un-necessary shot because Edwards was going well by this time. Yet these are the occasions when logic departs and the 'red mist' takes over. A batsman can mutter under his breath, 'Now stay here. Occupy the crease. The runs are coming quickly enough', but before he has drawn breath again he has slogged the ball up in the air aiming for a boundary. Such exits from the field bring cat-calls from the crowd, or patronising words of condolence, both of which are equally unacceptable. What happens in fact when a batsman gets himself out, pulls the cord to release his own guillotine, is that he lashes himself with his tongue and finds a dark corner of the dressing room in which to 'die'.

Marsh soon touched one to the wicket-keeper. 195 for 6 but then the innings swung in an unexpected direction. Asif brought on leg-spinner Wasim Raja to bowl and in the last ten overs Australia added 79 runs. Edwards could scarcely believe his luck, and he was helped in the assault by Jeff Thomson and Max Walker. The sharpest singles were taken; not even the return of Pakistan fast bowling could stem the flow, and facing an ultimate target of 279 to win, Pakistan must have realised that they would have to be at their best with the bat to win.

The sight of England batsmen cowering from the pace of Jeff Thomson, which was our armchair viewing during the winter, has obviously created some bloodthirsty appetites around the country. At least the roars suggested more than the mere anticipation of watching truly fast bowlers go about their destructive business. Oddly enough it was Majid Khan, now opening for his country, who first alerted the British cricketing fraternity to the speed of Jeff Thomson. Thomson's first Test was against Pakistan in 1972. Majid immediately reported that this was the man who would be the quickest in the world within a few seasons. Now they were face to face again.

Majid is an important figure in this side. He possesses talent which can cope with any variation of bowling on any quality wicket. Little else need be said to enhance that reputation. What brings out this talent is the challenge.

A few seasons ago he teased the Glamorgan bowlers in the dressing room at Derby. It was an argument about how much footwork is required in batting. Majid issued the challenge, 'I will play you all with feet together, standing still.' So out to the net they went, to find a wet turning pitch. For half an hour, with just a swivel of his feet, he played all manner of strokes to his own huge delight. The lifting cutters of Don Shepherd he dropped down or pulled through mid-wicket. Many balls he let pass the off-stump, and with an amusing but skilful exhibition of timing, he proved what he set out to prove, that footwork was not always necessary for batting . . . *for him.*

He would relish the assault of Lillee and Thomson because he would want to prove his courage and ability by taming them. Yet he would not prepare for his innings, say like Geoff Boycott, with the professional's attention to detail—padding taped on to the index finger of the right hand to prevent jarring; sweat band on wrists to rub the perspiration out of the eyelashes rather than have 'drops' before the eyes; extra padding on the pad-straps to remove the possibility of discomfort during a long innings. None of these preliminaries interest Majid. That day at Headingley he more likely donned a plain thigh pad, gloves and leg-guards and added the touch of individuality, which separates him from the masses—a stained off-white brimmed hat. He strolled to the middle with the pert, immaculate Sadiq at his side.

This was Thomson's first official bowl in England and far from being the tornado advertised, he required eleven balls to complete the first over. Umpire Tom Spencer was forced to signal four no-balls for overstepping the popping crease, and one for a wide. The crowd relished the humiliation and Thomson rewarded them at the conclusion of the over with an indecent gesture. However, 8 overs, 1 wicket for 25 runs was still reasonable enough by the end.

It was his more illustrious partner Dennis Lillee who did the damage. Sadiq was his first victim, yorked. Zaheer mishooked Thomson, Mushtaq was caught at cover, a careless slashing shot, and it was left to Majid and his captain Asif to take the score on from 68 for 3 to 104 for 4, well up with the prescribed scoring rate. Majid's stroke play sent the flags waving. Lillee was hooked and driven for fours and two cuts off Mallett were executed so late, yet with so much power, that they travelled up the hill to the boundary, one for four and the other for three. He attempted to swing Mallett to the leg side, got a touch that only few could have detected and walked instantly back to the pavilion. Once again to take on the highest class of opposition he had plumbed the depth of his ability and come up with absolute gems. His departure ended all hope, in spite of a flourish by Asif with Wasim Raja. The truth could not be avoided. Dennis Lillee was due back on the scene in the 43rd over.

Straightway he blasted Asif's off stump out of the ground and then made a complete mess of the tail.

His speed and the unerring line he maintains just on or around the off stump are going to make him a terribly difficult bowler to manage later in the year, and when you watch his legs carry him strongly over a fast, rhythmical run-up, black mane flying, the back suddenly arched and the ball projected out of a flying pivot, you wonder just what courage it took to come back to the game having suffered three stress fractures of the spine. The former Yorkshire bowler Bob Appleyard understood, awarding Lillee the Man of the Match award—and who would quarrel with that?

EDGBASTON; Saturday, June 7th, 1975

Group A: New Zealand beat East Africa by 181 runs

NEW ZEALAND

G. M. Turner	not out	171
J. F. M. Morrison	c & b Nana	14
G. P. Howarth	b Quaraishy	20
J. H. Parker	c Zulfiqar, b Sethi	66
B. F. Hastings	c Sethi, b Zulfiqar	8
K. J. Wadsworth	b Nagenda	10
R. J. Hadlee	not out	6
Extras (b 1, lb 8, w 5)		14
	Total (5 wkts)	309

Innings closed.
Did not bat: B. J. McKechnie, D. R. Hadlee, H. J. Howarth, R. O. Collinge.

Fall of wickets: 1-51, 2-103, 3-252, 4-278, 5-292.
Bowling: Nagenda 9-1-50-1, Frasat 9-0-50-0, Nana 12-2-34-1,
Sethi 10-1-51-1, Zulfiqar 12-0-71-1, Quraishy 8-0-39-1.

EAST AFRICA

Frasat Ali	st Wadsworth, b H. J. Howarth	45
Sam Walusimba	b D. R. Hadlee	15
Ramesh Sethi	run out	1
Shiraz Sumar	b D. R. Hadlee	4
Jawahir Shah	c & b H. J. Howarth	5
Harilal R. Shah	lbw H. J. Howarth	0
Mehmood Quraishy	not out	16
Zulfiqar Ali	b D. R. Hadlee	30
H. McLeod	b Collinge	5
P. G. Nana	not out	1
Extras (lb 5, nb 1)		6
	Total (8 wkts)	128

Innings closed.
Did not bat: John Nagenda.
Fall of wickets: 1-30, 2-32, 3-36, 4-59, 5-59, 6-84, 7-121,
8-126.
Bowling: Collinge 12-5-23-1, R. J. Hadlee 12-6-10-0,
McKechnie 12-2-39-0, D. R. Hadlee 12-1-21-3, H. J. Howarth
12-3-29-3.
New Zealand won by 181 runs.
Umpires: H. D. Bird, A. E. Fagg.
Man of the Match: G. M. Turner.
Adjudicator: D. Kenyon.

The concept of the Prudential Cup allowed for the
inclusion of two countries inexperienced in international
cricket competition, yet soundly enough based to develop
with encouragement. The team representing East Africa
on this roasting hot June day was composed of six
Kenyans, two Zambians, two Ugandans and one
Tanzanian, quite a mixture, as indeed there is a medley
of races in the squad—ten of Asian descent, two Africans
and two Europeans, Hamish McLeod, a Slazenger representative on the copperbelt, in Zambia, and Donald
Pringle, a landscape consultant from Kenya.

Yet forces joined did not bring strength on this
particular day, nor is there a sign that East Africa can do

Absurdly casual Clive Lloyd goes for a stroll down the wicket and wafts the ball for a boundary in the Final

Umpire Bird consults Spencer before giving a controversial decision in Gary Gilmour's favour against Clive Lloyd in the Cup Final

Prudential Cup Final. Fredericks hooks Lillee for 6—but rubber studs can prove treacherous in the morning

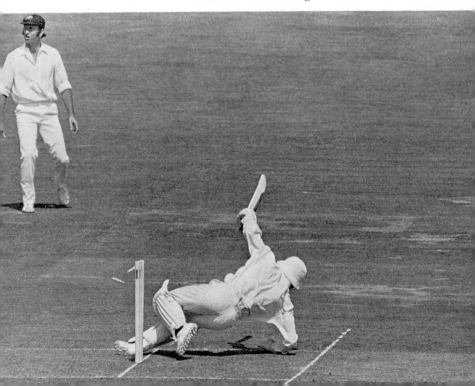

more than chase leather while they are here. This is the evidence after their chastening first match.

Running into Glenn Turner in full flow is not the happiest introduction to cricket in England. They are used to one-day cricket but in the field in the morning they were unable to pick up the half chances which might just have given New Zealand something to think about. New Zealand have a genuine reputation in one-day cricket. Not for the first time they won the Australian Gillette tournament, beating Western Australia quite easily in the final. They then went on to beat MCC handsomely at Melbourne. Back in New Zealand they again had the better of two one-day games against Mike Denness's side.

Turner's opening partnership with Morrison took the score just past fifty and at lunch New Zealand were 145 for 2 in 40 overs, getting on for a rate of 4 an over. The left arm spinner Nana should have caught and bowled Turner when he had scored only 16, and indeed had mid-off moved a little more smartly he might have gone to a catch at 27. Nana was by far the best bowler, 12 overs—2 maidens—34 runs for 1 wicket. The rest of the attack was medium-paced and none too accurate. The fielding was not up to it and when Turner was joined by his Worcestershire team-mate John Parker the grand total of 309 for 5 always looked likely. Incidentally Turner's 171 was the highest score ever made in a one-day international match but it fell short by two of the 173 scored by Gordon Greenidge at Amersham in 1973 (Benson & Hedges Competition). He and Parker added 149 in 23 overs.

East Africa had to endure the start they most feared though Frasat and Walusimbi appeared to be confident in defence. It was surprising when the latter was bowled by Dayle Hadlee. McKechnie hit the stumps direct to run out Sethi and Hadlee bowled Sumar. Then with the score on 59 there was momentary excitement when

B

Hedley Howarth trapped the two Shahs in consecutive balls. 59 for 5.

Frasat put together the most sturdy resistance, a 39-over fight to make 45 runs, once stepping down the wicket to strike Howarth for six. He was stumped when he tried to repeat the act of unexpected violence.

Will East Africa stand up better to the Indians at Headingley on Wednesday next? It will do them a power of good if they can.

OLD TRAFFORD; Saturday, June 7th, 1975

Group B: West Indies beat Sri Lanka by 9 wickets

SRI LANKA

R. Fernando	c Murray, b Julien	4
B. Warnapura	c Murray, b Boyce	8
A. Tennekoon	c Murray, b Julien	0
D. Heyn	c Lloyd, b Roberts	2
M. Tissera	c Kallicharran, b Julien	14
D. Mendis	c Murray, b Boyce	8
A. Ranasinghe	b Boyce	0
M. Pieris	c Lloyd, b Julien	3
M. Opatha	b Roberts	11
S. De Silva	c Lloyd, b Holder	21
L. Kaluperuma	not out	6
Extras (b 3, lb 3, nb 3)		9
	Total	86

Overs: 37.2.

Fall of wickets: 1-5, 2-5, 3-16, 4-21, 5-41, 6-41, 7-42, 8-48, 9-58.

Bowling: Roberts 12-5-16-2, Julien 12-3-20-4, Boyce 8-1-22-3, Gibbs 4-0-17-0, Holder 1.2-0-2-1.

WEST INDIES

R. C. Fredericks	c Warnapura, b De Silva	33
D. Murray	not out	30
A. Kallicharran	not out	19
Extras (b 2, lb 1, w 1, nb 1)		5
	Total (1 wkt)	87

Overs: 20.4.
Did not bat: R. Kanhai, C. Lloyd, V. Richards, B. Julien,
K. Boyce, V. Holder, A. Roberts, L. Gibbs.
Fall of wickets: 1-52.
Bowling: Opatha 4-0-19-0, Pieris 2-0-13-0, De Silva 8-1-33-1,
Kaluperuma 6.4-1-17-0.
West Indies won by 9 wickets.
Umpires: W. L. Budd, A. Jepson.
Man of the Match: B. Julien.
Adjudicator: R. Tattersall.

At least none of the Prudential competitors can utter complaint about the weather. Manchester was ablaze with sunshine: West Indians and Sri Lankans were at ease, even if the Mancunians themselves were too hot for comfort and forced to down one or two pints of beer more than usual. Possibly there was little else to claim the undivided attentions of those cognoscenti of the one-day game. At half-past three the entertainment was over. Sri Lanka put in to bat by Clive Lloyd were shot out for 86 and only managed to get the wicket of Roy Fredericks in return.

They had the sympathy of the many British players and administrators who have an affection for the country and its cricketers (the writer being one). They have come in search of success which will assist their application for full membership of the International Cricket Conference. If they get that, it will complete years of diligent service by all sorts of people—soldiers, civil administrators, missionaries, businessmen, planters and schoolteachers who helped the game spread through the island from its first strongholds in Colombo, Kandy and Galle. It has been played up country where tea plantations were carved out of the jungle and pitches were levelled by hand, often in rocky mountainous country. Planters would take their teams by cart fully twenty miles or more for a day's cricket. Cricket is a popular game for everyone, a truly national sport, and deserves recognition.

Fortunately Sri Lanka lies half way between Australia and Britain (as the ships fly), and much of their cricket has been gleaned from visitors. MCC teams call regularly. Test players go out early in the morning to schools and address young children. Players such as Gamini Goonesena, Stanley Jayasinghe, Clive Inman, Laddy Outschoorn and Dan Piachaud are among those who learned their game in Ceylon and who played in the County Championship in Britain.

When I learned of this débâcle at Old Trafford my thoughts returned to that Royal occasion at Lord's when all the teams met. I lunched that day with 'Dusty' Miller the Sri Lanka representative at Lord's and some of the players. The urgency of their questions suggested doubt and dispute in the camp as to how 60-over cricket should be played. Perhaps they were exaggerating the difficulties of strategy. Playing ability was no problem. I was prepared to underwrite that. All Sri Lanka needs to go ahead is recognition by the ICC and greater scope at their grounds to hold major Test matches. What no one could advise was how to bat well against the West Indies on this particular day in June when the ball moved about at Old Trafford.

Bernard Julien opened up and wobbled the new ball about for twelve overs without a break. He had done irrevocable damage when he gave way to the remainder of that formidable attack, Andy Roberts, Keith Boyce, Lance Gibbs, and Vanburn Holder. Fernando went for 4, caught behind, and Tennekoon, the captain, in similar fashion. This was a grievous blow because much faith was invested in his technique. He has scored two centuries against the Indians, one against MCC and another against Clive Lloyd's West Indians in Colombo.

Julien eventually took 4 for 20 and then Boyce came on first change to take 3 for 22. It was all too simple. Yet at 48 for 8, when the rout was almost over, there was a determined effort by De Silva and Opatha to salvage a

small corner of pride. The accident rate had been high—
Julien had Tissera taken at second slip: Mendis was
Murray's fourth victim behind the stumps: Boyce yorked
Ranasinghe.

As if they were not beset by enough problems, Sri
Lanka had to face demonstrators who ran on to the field
as David Heyn walked to the crease. Eight men squatted
beneath their banners! 'Racists', 'Anti-apartheid' they
proclaimed, messages seemingly aimed at affairs in Sri
Lanka. The police whistled them off too quickly for
anyone to be able to establish their loyalties.

De Silva and Kalumperuma bowled their spinners with
some accuracy in the West Indian innings. De Silva, the
leg-spinner, got Fredericks caught at backward point but
it was useful practice taken by the Guyanan left-hander
who is the only member of his side not currently engaged
in the English county circuit.

In the few days between matches there came an
announcement from the Surrey County Cricket Club that
tickets had been sold out for the Group B match
Australia versus West Indies, a week away, and that
there was no need to turn up unless you had one. 'The
match was sold out before the competition started,' so
the statement ran. 'There is no standing room and people
without tickets will definitely not be admitted.' If only
this amazing weather will hold.

Advance sales for the Prudential Cup Final on June
21st now total £50,000, and indeed on Sunday, Monday
and Tuesday the weather remains outrageously hot and
dry, the ball runs fast over outfields all over the country
and on the big grounds the dried-up herringbone pattern
of drainage shows through the baked earth.

Pre-match bookings for the game on Wednesday
between West Indies and Pakistan are most disappointing.
Leslie Deakins, the Warwickshire secretary, said 'We
certainly have the population in the area for this match.
We must hope for a fine day and that the crowds roll up.'

That message, in the light of what transpired both on and off the field, in that particular game, turned out to be the most unfounded touch of pessimism of the whole competition. There was no one more pleased than Leslie Deakins himself when he arrived at Edgbaston on Wednesday, June 11th, to find the sun shining and crowds clamouring at his gate.

EDGBASTON; Wednesday, June 11th, 1975

Group B: West Indies beat Pakistan by 1 wicket

PAKISTAN

Sadiq Mohammad	c Kanhai, b Julien	7
Majid Khan	c Murray, b Lloyd	60
Zaheer Abbas	lbw, b Richards	31
Mushtaq Mohammad	b Boyce	55
Wasim Raja	b Roberts	58
Javed Miandad	run out	24
Pervez Mir	run out	4
Wasim Bari	not out	1
Sarfraz Nawaz	not out	0
Extras (b 1, lb 15, w 4, nb 6)		26
Total (7 wkts)		266

Innings closed.
Did not bat: Asif Masood, Naseer Malik.
Fall of wickets: 1-21, 2-83, 3-140, 4-202, 5-249, 6-263, 7-265.
Bowling: Roberts 12-1-47-1, Julien 12-1-41-1, Boyce 12-2-44-1, Holder 12-3-56-0, Richards 4-0-21-1, Lloyd 8-1-31-1.

WEST INDIES

R. C. Fredericks	lbw, b Sarfraz	12
C. G. Greenidge	c Wasim Bari, b Sarfraz	4
A. I. Kallicharran	c Wasim Bari, b Sarfraz	16
R. B. Kanhai	b Naseer Malik	24
C. H. Lloyd	c Wasim Bari, b Javed	53
I. V. A. Richards	c Zaheer, b Pervez	13
B. D. Julien	c Javed, b Asif	18
D. L. Murray	not out	61
K. D. Boyce	b Naseer Malik	7
V. A. Holder	c Pervez, b Sarfraz	16

A. M. E. Roberts   not out   24
     Extras (lb 10, w 1, nb 8)   19

            Total (9 wkts)   267

59.4 overs.
Fall of wickets: 1-6, 2-31, 3-36, 4-84, 5-99, 6-145, 7-151, 8-166, 9-203.
Bowling: Asif 12-1-64-1, Sarfraz 12-1-44-4, Nasser 12-2-42-2, Pervez 9-1-42-1, Javed 12-0-46-1, Mushtaq 2-0-7-0, Wasim Raja 0.4-0-3-0.
West Indies won by 1 wicket.
Umpires: J. G. Langridge, D. J. Constant.
Man of the Match: Sarfraz Nawaz.
Adjudicator: T. W. Graveney.

It is a rare sporting experience which makes the heart of a neutral onlooker leap about. The bare facts from Edgbaston are that West Indies scored 267 for 9 wickets to beat Pakistan's 266 for 7, but my word, there was more to this day than that.

This will be recalled as one of the great games of cricket.

To have played in it for either side will be reason enough to puff with pride long after they have hung up their boots, to settle their grandchildren around them, and say 'Now I want to tell you about an extraordinary game of cricket, played at Edgbaston in Birmingham on June 11th, 1975.'

The story began for Pakistan two days before. Their captain Asif Iqbal was admitted to hospital in Birmingham for a minor but painful haemorrhoid operation and withdrew from the side, handing over the captaincy to Majid Khan. This was an immeasurable loss. Asif is one of the finest exponents of one-day cricket. His batting can supply the surge of brilliant stroke play; his medium fast bowling was very much part of Pakistan's strategy and as a fielder he was bound to set the sparkling example. One was mindful too that it was at Edgbaston in 1971 that Pakistan plundered England for 608 for 7.

The benign wicket remains but their chances are slimmer without Asif.

A second absentee restricted them further. Imran Khan, Majid's cousin, was locked in a battle with the examiners at Oxford University. He would be missed as an all-rounder, more especially his lively seam bowling. It meant that Majid had two fast bowlers of experience, Asif Masood and Sarfraz Nawaz, two others medium-paced, Naseer Malik and Pervez Mir. Presuming they all bowled their allocation of twelve overs each, it left another twelve to be shared between the leg spinners Mushtaq, Javed Miandad, and Wasim Raja. The captain would need a shade of luck to make it work. Compare the West Indies line-up—Roberts, arguably the fastest bowler in the world, Boyce and Vanburn Holder, both genuinely fast and experienced; Bernard Julien an established Test player and a useful variation with his left arm over the wicket style.

Then Clive Lloyd had an option. If it was medium fast bowling required, he could put himself on, generally neat and tidy, short of a length. Then lurking in the background was off-spinner Vivian Richards, an occasional bowler, but useful. Lance Gibbs was selected in their fourteen, but omitted.

If Pakistan won, the West Indies would need to beat Australia in that sell-out match at the Oval on Saturday next to reach the semi-finals. Even then, Pakistan might just have nosed them out of place on a superior scoring rate. So there was much to play for, as I gathered when I got to the ground just as the first over was being delivered.

At Edgbaston it is possible to walk around a path outside the stands where there is no sight of the game. It was along this that I hurried to the press box. The noise was deafening and most certainly foreign. A crescendo of roars, from the bottom of the scale to the top, told me that Andy Roberts was racing in to the

accompaniment of a vast West Indian chorus. It was
followed by a brief split second of silent anticipation, a
click of bat on ball, and then a gush of counter cheering
and chattering from the Pakistanis. Spectators arriving a
little late raced up steps to the stands, argued with
gatemen, shouted at friends, jabbered away at anybody—a
magnificent confusion of dialects. If I closed my eyes I
could have been in the Kensington Oval, Barbados, or
Karachi, a feeling confirmed when I took in my first
view of the serried ranks. A coloured crowd indeed,
two-thirds of them West Indian or Pakistani, and
Edgbaston's terraces, so often grey and deserted, had
disappeared beneath the stamping feet of 18,000 spectators all caught up in the joy or pain of following the
fluctuating fortunes. As a privileged outsider one could
find oneself literally trapped in one of the many large
green and white flags waved about in a frenzy, or feel
one's eardrums shattered by West Indians banging beer
cans to the rhythms of war.

Pakistan had won the toss and batted, but lost Sadiq
when the score was just 21. Then Majid and Zaheer
eased their way out of a possible crisis, yet found it
difficult to increase the tempo when they wanted to.
Keith Boyce and Vanburn Holder restricted them both
at this stage with skilful defensive bowling just short of
a length on middle and leg stumps.

Flashing drives soon revealed the easy nature of the
wicket. Majid sorted out his footwork which had looked
stiff and imprecise to begin with and, ball by ball, he
grew into a more formidable threat to West Indies. The
game was truly alight.

Fredericks moved like a cat low to the ground to
snatch up a couple of sizzling shots in his prehensile
fingers and flipped the ball back over the stumps from
cover point. Keith Boyce let his arm go from the outfield
like a human sling; over seventy or eighty yards the ball
travelled at a level a foot over stump high, almost

defying even the safest second run. The Pakistan batsmen knew that, if put under pressure, Boyce is the sort of athlete who might next time pick-up on the run and add a leaping throw, all in one movement. Then, of course, there was the king-cat of the jungle, Clive Lloyd. Zaheer drove Boyce powerfully wide of Lloyd at mid-on. The captain turned and raced over the bone hard outfield like one of the great coloured sprinters burning up the hundred metre track. The ball was arrested on the boundary line, and winged back to where it belonged, straight into Deryck Murray's gloves, with one vicious revolution of a flaying arm. The intensity, the sheer quality of it all (and it was only half an hour after mid-day —seven and a half hours to go!) left one shaking one's head. It is easy to exaggerate sometimes, but even more unforgivable not to recognise moments of true excellence when you see them and savour them briefly before they die with the next ball, or, in this case, with the next day.

Clive Lloyd next made a decision which surprised many. He called upon Viv Richards, the part-time off spinner, to bowl to these two fine players whose eyes were well set. In his first over he got Zaheer lbw as he carelessly tried to pull a shortish ball which did not turn. Roberts returned to test Mushtaq, but to no avail. Majid lashed Lloyd high and wide of mid-on, then fell to a ball of higher bounce, caught behind for 60.

Mushtaq's steadiness settled the innings at a time when Wasim Raja was prepared to hurl his bat at almost anything. Had he mistaken the 37th over for the last?

It was at this moment that Lloyd and Julien settled to bowl well. Mushtaq's timing kept his score on the move however. He even charged down the wicket to Boyce who considered this such an insult to the fast bowling trade that, with the tiger in his eye, he let go a 'beamer' which narrowly by-passed Mushtaq's moustache and got the message home. Kallicharan dropped Wasim Raja just before Boyce produced the most perfect yorker to dismiss Mushtaq, all leading up to a last over chaos which included two run-outs. Vanburn Holder was the bowler and the central figure. Mir went at the striker's end and Miandad at the bowler's. Miandad, 17, had played with pleasing confidence and it is easy to understand why hopes have arisen in Pakistan for his successful future in the game.

The final total of 266 allowed Pakistan the satisfaction of knowing that the West Indies could not afford to be frivolous about it.

Yet the Caribbean cricketers are unpredictable souls. Fredericks, Greenidge, Kallicharran and Kanhai tried to launch themselves with extravagant stroke play, a haste quite irrelevant to the target, to the bowling, to the wicket—the lot. To see it was to be reminded of words penned by the West Indian journalist, Tony Cozier, of his countrymen's temperament which mostly brings them strength and individuality, but occasionally destroys them.

'The aim of every young West Indian cricketer is universal but pursued more zealously than elsewhere: to hit the ball harder and bowl it faster than anyone else.

'No player feels the chafing against the grain of his nature more acutely than a West Indian, contained for over after over; no player feels less delight in stock bowling—steady, economical, medium-pace, tick-tock stuff. Other men can jog around sturdily and usefully like pit ponies; the West Indian craves the padding grace and the striking power of the panther.'

Thus departed Greenidge, Fredericks and Kallicharran for 36 runs, though I would not wish to devalue the performance of Sarfraz who had taken 3 wickets for 10 runs in 3.4 overs.

Clive Lloyd changed the mood, Kanhai too had just got the message when he hacked a wide full pitch on to his stumps. Richards and Boyce offered yet more feverish renderings, but Julien lined up with the sane and resolute, and joined his captain in an important stand.

It was the young leg-spinner, Javed Miandad, who beat Lloyd with a perfectly pitched googly. The umpire, John Langridge, responded positively to a loud shout for a catch by 'keeper Wasim Bari. Lloyd expressed his surprise and annoyance; Langridge was in no doubt at all.

Holder then batted with relish for the job but at 203 for 9 he was gone too and Pakistan had virtually won the match fair and square. So what followed was a near-miracle borne of the very equation of possibilities which can make the game of cricket the perfect drama. There was a peculiar agony reserved for Pakistan on this occasion, and post-mortem does nothing but rub in the peppers. Somehow they failed to remove Deryck Murray, a · batsman of orthodoxy and correctness, and Andy Roberts, no recognised batsman at all. These two put on 64 for the last wicket to win the match on the 4th ball of the 6oth and final over.

Majid first took an understandable decision, one above criticism. He resolved to try to bowl out the last man by allowing Sarfraz to use up his overs. With 5 overs left, Sarfraz, Javed and Naseer had finished their quota. Roberts had defended in the main with the forward lunge, while Murray selected his scoring shots with perfect nerve and judgement.

These two came together in the 46th over. With 6 overs to go, 29 were wanted, and the West Indian crowd which had fallen silent began the rumblings of what was to be a giant eruption. 16 runs were required from 4 overs. Pervez Mir bowled a maiden. 16 runs from 3 overs. 10 runs off 2. So the last over arrived with 5 runs for victory—Andy Roberts taking strike.

But who was to bowl? Asif Masood had finished, Pervez Mir had 3 overs to go but had bowled the last over at the other end. Mushtaq might be the man; he had already turned his arm over for two overs conceding seven runs. Or there was one alternative, the lower trajectory leg spin of Wasim Raja. Wasim was chosen, though he attempted to bowl medium-paced seamers. Two leg-byes came behind the wicket on the on-side (one of them an overthrow)—poor Pakistan were suffering now, and were probably losing the game for the first time in seven hours cricket. First two runs, then one—all over, and it was simply left to Tom Graveney to judge Sarfraz Nawaz the Man of the Match, a consolation deserved. Only two fine sides could make a match such as this had been.

It is possible that Majid could have catered for a stronger last over than that bowled by Wasim Raja but, in truth, it was the batting which won it, not the bowling which lost it.

Deryck Murray is one of the more orthodox sons of the Caribbean, a neat looking man, tidy in his play too. He hit the ball particularly well through the off-side field on this day, and hooked swiftly when the bouncer was sent down to blast him out. He was not to be moved. It was a demonstration of personal resolution. His mouth must have been dry with the million visions of success and failure which raced through his mind and, by the end, his very soul must have been stretched by the constant temptation to abandon restraint and rush for his shots. That innings said more about his character than a hundred visits to a psychiatrist's couch.

TRENT BRIDGE; Wednesday, June 11th, 1975

Group A: England beat New Zealand by 80 runs

ENGLAND		
D. L. Amiss	b Collinge	16
J. A. Jameson	c Wadsworth, b Collinge	11

K. W. R. Fletcher	run out	131
F. C. Hayes	lbw, b R. J. Hadlee	34
M. H. Denness	c Morrison, b D. R. Hadlee	37
A. W. Greig	b D. R. Hadlee	9
C. M. Old	not out	20
Extras (lb 6, w 1, nb 1)		8

Total (6 wkts) 266

Innings closed.
Did not bat: A. P. E. Knott, D. L. Underwood, G. G. Arnold, P. Lever.
Fall of wickets: 1-27, 2-28, 3-111, 4-177, 5-200, 6-266.
Bowling: Collinge 12-2-43-2, R. J. Hadlee 12-2-66-1, D. R. Hadlee 12-1-55-2, McKechnie 12-2-38-0, Howarth 12-2-56-0.

NEW ZEALAND

J. F. M. Morrison	c Old, b Underwood	55
G. M. Turner	b Lever	12
B. G. Hadlee	c Old, b Greig	19
J. M. Parker	b Greig	1
B. F. Hastings	c Underwood, b Old	10
K. J. Wadsworth	b Arnold	25
R. J. Hadlee	b Old	0
B. J. McKechnie	c Underwood, b Greig	27
D. R. Hadlee	c Arnold, b Greig	20
H. J. Howarth	not out	1
R. O. Collinge	b Underwood	6
Extras (b 1, lb 4, w 1, nb 4)		10

Total 186

Innings closed.
Fall of wickets: 1-30, 2-83, 3-91, 4-95, 5-129, 6-129, 7-129, 8-177, 9-180.
Bowling: Arnold 12-3-35-1, Lever 12-0-37-1, Old 12-2-29-2, Underwood 12-2-30-2, Greig 12-0-45-4.
England won by 80 runs.
Umpires: W. E. Alley, T. W. Spencer.
Man of the Match: K. W. R. Fletcher.
Adjudicator: J. Hardstaff.

New Zealand cricketers have recently made themselves a reputation for expertise in one-day cricket, and they confronted England at Trent Bridge with their first serious test of the competition.

Reference is made earlier to New Zealand's winning of

the Australasian Gillette Cup, beating Western Australia without too much trouble in the final. They overcame MCC too at Melbourne.

Glenn Turner is their new captain, now that Bevan Congdon has withdrawn because of business pressures, and Turner's experience with Worcestershire through many seasons of success in limited-over cricket was bound to serve New Zealand well in pursuit of the Prudential prize.

New Zealand *v* England battles have been going on since A. H. H. Gilligan led MCC out there in 1929–30. The record rather cruelly emphasises the quality of the game in that part of the world. Of 45 Tests England have won 22, 23 have been drawn. Never have New Zealand left the field victors. Yet in 1973, in England, they came closer than they would care to remember. When they had to get 479 for victory on this same Trent Bridge ground, they managed 440. Then in the second of the three Tests at Lord's they outplayed England almost throughout. Amassing 551 for 9, Congdon declared their first innings closed and they bowled England out for 253. The follow-on was enforced. One man stood between them and this first long dreamed of victory, Keith Fletcher. Indeed Fletcher has been the curse of New Zealand hopes more than once. In that Test he accumulated, with scarcely a hint of anxiety or flourish, 178 in the second innings.

At Auckland last winter, 1975, England were 153 for 3 and then 419 for 4 with Fletcher making 216. Small wonder the Essex captain approached this Nottingham task with a measure of confidence! Rescuing England from a shaky start he showed off the Fletcher which so many of his supporters would love to see more often on the Test field, resolute at first, but opening out his arm-swing into wider and wider arcs. These strokes made him a memorable 131. With much affection the playing fraternity have picked up his Essex nick-name 'Gnome'.

So read the *Daily Mirror* headline: 'The "Gnome" is England's Superman'. New Zealand appeared demoralised. Morrison made 55 but they failed to reach the target of 267 by 80 runs. They were not truly in the hunt at any stage.

Without a doubt, success over England will come to them one day, and it is obviously in the interests of the game of cricket in that country that they do. New Zealand Test players in the 1970s pack in more cricket than they ever did. In many ways, most noticeably in technique, they have acquired a good deal more sophistication than their cavalier forefathers ever envisaged. International commitments are heavier and have obviously assisted the improvement. Of New Zealand's eight victories in 114 Tests, over forty-five years, five have come since 1968.

In many ways they labour against the geographical odds. Only three million people inhabit the country, and the game of cricket exists on the meagre base of Saturday to Saturday club competition. From the senior grades come the best players into first-class cricket. Standards are erratic, pitches are often matting in country places.

Perhaps New Zealand cricket is dimmed by the more glossy prestige sport, rugby football. Very few sons of New Zealand escape either the sweet smell of a rugger ball in the hand or the roughness of a tackle. I recall playing against New Zealand at Cardiff Arms Park in 1965. Glamorgan's cricket field, at Cardiff Arms Park in those days, nestled under the shadows of the tall rugby stand on the other side of which thousands of hymn-singing Welshmen used to watch the scarlet jerseys in action in the winter. The changing rooms for both rugby and cricket were the same, dark rooms smelling of wintergreen linament even in the summer.

Light rain stopped play on this occasion, and during the break some New Zealanders had seized upon two rugby balls, tucked their white flannels in their socks and rushed on to the hallowed turf for a kick-around. Rain was falling quite hard when they were guided acrossfield to the corner where Bob Deans, the All Black centre, claimed he had scored a try to level scores with Wales in 1905. The referee turned it down. Wales won and there was not one of these cricketers of generations later who needed reminding of the event. Cricket in New Zealand is a light-weight sport by comparison.

At Nottingham, because there was a mist hanging over the ground, which skirts the River Trent, New Zealand put England in and this looked entirely justified for a time. Collinge struck first when in the seventh over he moved the ball enough to beat Amiss's drive and bowl him. In his next over he had Jameson well taken behind the wicket by Wadsworth. Two down for 28. Yet Hayes joining Fletcher put on 83 for the third wicket in 23 overs before he mistimed a pull shot and was lbw. Mike Denness is thought to be very much on trial in this Prudential series, indeed he has been under the constant scrutiny of critics ever since he took over the England captaincy from Ray Illingworth. Winter tour defeats in Australia did not strengthen his cause, yet he has come up with plenty of runs for England, certainly as many as other players in the side. His later innings, after a torrid time, said much for the strength of his personal qualities. Too many scathing remarks about his personal character lowered the standards of cricket writing beyond all good sense, yet he answered them with 188 in the 6th Test v Australia, 181 in the first New Zealand Test at Auckland and 59 not out in the second at Christchurch.

In this Prudential match he struck his best form again though only for a short time. He and Fletcher put on 66 runs in 16 overs. Greig failed as he has done so frequently this season, but nothing could stop Fletcher. His hundred came in the 55th over; altogether he put away 13 boundaries and eventually was run-out off the last ball of the innings.

The wicket of Glenn Turner is priceless if it comes in

the first half hour. Peter Lever contributed that by bowling the New Zealand captain when the score was 30. Morrison and Barry Hadlee still kept the game alive and at 80 for 1 the situation promised a close scramble towards the end. Yet it was spin bowling by Greig and Underwood which suddenly transformed the score to 95–4. Morrison, who had hung on valiantly, lofted Underwood to square leg, so unhitching the anchor and sending New Zealand downhill to a surprise but comprehensive defeat.

HEADINGLEY; Wednesday, June 11th, 1975

Group A: India beat East Africa by 10 wickets

EAST AFRICA		
Frasat Ali	b Abid Ali	12
Sam Walusimba	lbw, b Abid Ali	16
Praful Mehta	run out	12
Yunus Badat	b Bedi	1
Jawahir Shah	b Amarnath	37
Harilal R. Shah	c Engineer, b Amarnath	0
Ramesh Sethi	c Gaekwad, b Madan Lal	23
Mehmood Quaraishy	run out	6
Zulfiqar Ali	not out	2
P. G. Nana	lbw, b Madan Lal	0
D. Pringle	b Madan Lal	2
Extras (lb 8, nb 1)		9
	Total	120

55.3 overs.
Fall of wickets: 1-27, 2-36, 3-37, 4-56, 5-56, 6-98, 7-116, 8-116, 9-116.
Bowling: Abid Ali 12-5-22-2, Madan Lal 9.3-2-15-3, Bedi 12-8-6-1, Venkat 12-4-29-0, Amarnath 10-0-39-2.

INDIA		
S. M. Gavaskar	not out	65
F. M. Engineer	not out	54
Extras (b 4)		4
	Total (no wkt)	123

29.5 overs.
Did not bat: A. D. Gaekwad, G. R. Viswanath, B. P. Patel,
E. D. Solkar, S. Abid Ali, Madan Lal Sharma, M. Amarnath,
S. Venkat, B. S. Bedi.
Bowling: Frasat 6-1-17-0, Pringle 3-0-14-0, Zulfiqar
11-3-32-0, Nana 4.5-0-36-0, Sethi 5-0-20-0.
India won by 10 wickets.
Umpires: H. D. Bird, A. Jepson.
Man of the Match: F. M. Engineer.
Adjudicator: J. G. Binks.

There was never going to be a way that East Africa
could challenge India at Headingley. Two messages had
got home to India by this time, one, that they were
honourbound to answer the call of the competition for
attacking cricket and, secondly, that the presence of
Bishen Bedi was essential to their side.

Bedi is considered to be one of the finest left arm
spinners in the world and to omit a world-class bowler,
as they did at Lord's, did appear to lack judgement. Yet
West Indies have a top class spinner in their ranks who
has not been chosen so far, Lance Gibbs. One can argue
that neither is likely to score many runs with the bat, but
the theory most likely to keep them out of their sides is
that medium-fast bowling is the more restrictive style in
limited-over cricket. I am not certain that this is true
when comparisons are made between spinners like Bedi
who can bowl to a strict pattern of field placings, and
fast medium bowlers of average talent like Abid Ali,
Madan Lal, Amarnath and Ghavri. Anyway Bedi tor-
mented the inexperienced East Africans, 12 overs, 8
maidens, 6 runs, 1 wicket.

The competition so far has been blessed with the most
perfect weather, sunny and warm, offering overseas
players conditions much more like their own at home
than the truly British green seaming wickets which they
probably all feared. It was no comfort to East Africa
however. Their talents are modest, though they do not

lack potential and if they have learned from this summer's experience in England then their inclusion in the competition is justified.

Against India a number of their batsmen showed lack of experience, though Jawahir and Sethi made a better job than most. Their score of 120 was unlikely to be enough and Gavaskar and Engineer sailed home to an easy victory. Farooq Engineer won the Man of the Match award, decided in his favour by another wicket keeper Jim Binks, formerly of Yorkshire and England. Engineer pulled a hamstring muscle at Lord's on June 7th and this prompted him to walk, not run, most of his singles against East Africa. This more than anything emphasised the great gulf in class between the two sides. An even sadder observation is that East African skipper Harilal has been out first ball in both matches so far.

THE OVAL; Wednesday, June 11th, 1975

Group B: Australia beat Sri Lanka by 52 runs

AUSTRALIA

R. B. McCosker	b De Silva	73
A. Turner	c Mendis, b De Silva	101
I. M. Chappell	b Kaluperuma	4
G. S. Chappell	c Opatha, b Pieris	50
K. D. Walters	c Tennekoon, b Pieris	59
J. R. Thomson	not out	9
R. W. Marsh	not out	9
Extras (lb 20, b 1, w 1, nb 1)		23
	Total (5 wkts)	328

Innings closed.

Did not bat: R. Edwards, M. H. N. Walker, D. K. Lillee, A. A. Mallett.

Fall of wickets: 1-182, 2-187, 3-191, 4-308, 5-308.

Bowling: Opatha 9-0-32-0, Pieris 11-0-68-2, Warnapura 9-0-40-0, Ranasinghe 7-0-55-0, De Silva 12-3-60-2, Kaluperuma 12-0-50-1.

SRI LANKA

S. Wettimuny	retired hurt	53
R. Fernando	b Thomson	22
B. Warnapura	st Marsh, b Mallett	31
D. Mendis	retired hurt	32
A. Tennekoon	b I. M. Chappell	48
M. Tissera	c Turner, b I. M. Chappell	52
A. Ranasinghe	not out	14
M. Pieris	not out	0
Extras (b 6, lb 8, w 8, nb 2)		24

Total (4 wkts) 276

Innings closed.

Did not bat: T. Opatha, S. De Silva, L. Kaluperuma.

Fall of wickets: 1-30, 2-84, 3-246, 4-268.

Bowling: Lillee 10-0-42-0, Thomson 12-5-22-1, Mallett 12-0-72-1, Walters 6-1-33-0, Walker 12-1-44-0, G. S. Chappell 4-0-25-0, I. M. Chappell 4-0-14-2.

Australia won by 52 runs.

Umpires: W. L. Budd, A. E. Fagg.

Man of the Match: A. Turner.

Adjudicator: L. B. Fishlock.

The hopes of Sri Lanka before they left home must have been more firmly based than those of East Africa. For many reasons Ceylon had competed with Indian sides as well as enticing major Test playing countries to visit them. The style of their batsmen especially suggests that they have been fired in the right sort of competitive game. Given fine weather and a 'following wind' there was always the probability that they would make a substantial total against someone. That they achieved this against Australia added a glow of satisfaction which I am sure quickly buzzed along the telephone wires to Colombo.

The West Indies had outclassed them and humiliated them at Old Trafford and it was with this experience in mind rather than any tactical intent that Tennekoon put Australia in to bat when he won the toss. At least the game would last most of the day this way around, even if they did fail against one of the finest attacks in the world.

Turner and McCosker launched the Australian innings with massive authority. Of the six bowlers presenting themselves for sacrifice, only Opatha, the opening seam bowler, imposed anything like restraint, and that in relative terms. Yet he was only called upon to send down 9 overs. If McCosker was less adventurous than his partner, it was perhaps only because he offered no chinks in defence. At lunch, after 34 overs, Turner had reached his hundred, McCosker was 69 and the total stood at 178. Turner struck one huge six on to the upper deck of the stand behind long-on. The fielding showed signs of falling apart under pressure, and the remainder of the day looked to be a straightforward academic exercise for the Australians.

The sun blazed down in the afternoon and for a while there was a permanent buzz of activity with wickets for a moment as frequent as runs. Turner went in the 36th over, failing to clear little Mendis's grasp at mid-off. McCosker followed in de Silva's next over, and when Ian Chappell played across the line in the 39th over, three wickets had fallen in eleven balls. Greg Chappell and Walters responded with arrogance—117 in 19 overs, the fielding now fraying at the edges.

So to the crease came the little men with no hope. The notorious Dennis Lillee duly positioned his four slips and a gully, but Wettimuny managed to touch one between them to get off the mark. Soon Fernando demonstrated how the bad ball should be despatched for four. The ground rang out to the sound of his bat and the Oval's 6,000 spectators warmed to the Sri Lankan cause, whether they were concerned or not. 23 runs were on the board in 5 overs but Fernando went at 30 when he dragged a ball from Thomson rather unluckily on to the wicket. Warnapura joined Wettimuny and the pace of run-getting did not slow down. 51 in 14 overs became 84 in 18. At tea, having lost Warnapura, Sri Lanka were 115 for 2; they had surprised many who did not appreciate how correctly and enterprisingly they can play.

It was after the interval that incidents occurred which attracted the attention of match reporters and made the headlines—'Terror Thommo', and 'Thommo's War'. Jeff Thomson dropped a short ball to Mendis who was 32 not out. It climbed high off the ground and struck Mendis on the side of the head.

The diminutive Sri Lankan crumpled and was carried off the field, then to St. Thomas's hospital. The ball was not terribly short and was well within the bounds of fair play. The crowd shouted 'Off, Off' and hounded Thomson in everything he attempted for the remainder of the match. Australian manager, Fred Bennett, made the obvious but most intelligent of a number of comments which were flying around after the game, 'What do you expect Thomson to do . . . bowl underarm?'

Yet Thomson was not finished with violence. Wettimuny, who had taken several painful blows from him, chopped the ball on to his foot, an incident which was sufficiently painful for him to require a runner, and then did precisely the same thing again. Whilst he was hopping about in agony, Thomson followed up, grabbed the ball, and threw down the wicket. It is perfectly within the laws to do so, but I am sure his unnecessary act of aggression made neither him nor his side any friends. Wettimuny, as it happened, was in his crease, but unable to bat on. Within minutes he had joined the queue at St. Thomas's!

Michael Tissera is a man I know well. He has often led Sri Lanka against MCC sides. A lean, stylish batsman, he harbours a deep determination, a true competitive spirit. With his captain Tennekoon, he put up the 200 in the 45th over. Ian Chappell rang the changes with his bowlers, but none looked likely to separate them; more to Sri Lanka's credit, they did not stem the flow of attacking strokes. They genuinely tried to win the match and left bowlers, like Mallett for example, with 72 runs taken off his 12 overs; Walker conceded 44 without taking a wicket. It was an immensely brave performance to get within 52 before defeat came.

The former Surrey and England batsman Laurie Fishlock awarded the Man of the Match prize to Alan Turner, but who knows if Mendis and Wettimuny had not been hurt what would have been the outcome. After all, a retirement in one-day cricket is tantamount to a wicket falling, though I suspect Australia are too fine a side to allow giant-killing at their expense. The miracle remains to all who watch these matches, that two sides from lands far away have actually been brought together in the name of cricket, to compete on the turf where it all started many years ago, and in magnificent day-long sunshine.

SATURDAY, JUNE 14th

Let us consider the group tables with two matches played by every team.

Group A	P	W	L	Pts
England	2	2	0	8
New Zealand	2	1	1	4
India	2	1	1	4
East Africa	2	0	2	0

Group B	P	W	L	Pts
Australia	2	2	0	8
West Indies	2	2	0	8
Pakistan	2	0	2	0
Sri Lanka	2	0	2	0

So what was at stake in this third and final preliminary set of matches? There was one crucial cup-tie, one outstanding match and, inevitably in this eight-man competition, two foregone conclusions. India and New Zealand met at Old Trafford to decide which one of them went forward to the semi-final. More spectacularly, at the Oval, Australia and West Indies joined in a battle awaited by partisans and uncommitted alike. Any cricket-lover in the world would surely want to see this one. However, neither side could lose its place in the semi-finals. England were expected to overcome East Africa as easily as Pakistan—already unluckily eliminated —should deal with Sri Lanka at Trent Bridge.

Announcements have come from the Oval via radio, television and newspaper that no one should present himself or herself at the Hobbs gates hoping to gain admission without a ticket. It only remains to point out that the losers of this encounter of giants will meet England in the semi-final at Headingley, and the winners play (at the Oval) the side that comes through the India v New Zealand tie.

Just to add spice to the occasion, Ladbrokes reported the following backing. After laying £10,000 in bets for India to beat New Zealand, they reduced the odds from 11–4 to 7–4. New Zealand are 4–9. The latest prices to win the Cup are: 7–4 West Indies; 15–8 Australia; 11–4 England; 11–1 New Zealand; 40–1 India.

OLD TRAFFORD; Saturday, June 14th, 1975

Group A: New Zealand beat India by 4 wickets

INDIA		
S. M. Gavaskar	c R. J. Hadlee, b D. R. Hadlee	12
F. M. Engineer	lbw, b R. J. Hadlee	24
A. D. Gaekwad	c Hastings, b R. J. Hadlee	37
G. R. Viswanath	lbw, b McKechnie	2
B. Patel	c Wadsworth, b H. J. Howarth	9
E. D. Solkar	c Wadsworth, b H. J. Howarth	13
S. Abid Ali	c H. J. Howarth, b McKechnie	70
Madan Lal	c & b McKechnie	20

S. M. Amarnath	c Morrison, b D. R. Hadlee	1
S. Venkataraghavan	not out	26
B. S. Bedi	run out	6
Extras (b 5, w 1, nb 4)		10

Total 230

Innings closed.

Fall of wickets: 1-17, 2-48, 3-59, 4-81, 5-94, 6-101, 7-156, 8-157, 9-217.

Bowling: Collinge 12-2-43-0, R. J. Hadlee 12-2-48-2, D. R. Hadlee 12-3-32-2, McKechnie 12-1-49-3, H. J. Howarth 12-0-48-2.

NEW ZEALAND

G. M. Turner	not out	114
J. F. M. Morrison	c Engineer, b Bedi	17
G. P. Howarth	run out	9
J. M. Parker	lbw, b Abid Ali	1
B. F. Hastings	c Solkar, b Amarnath	34
K. J. Wadsworth	lbw, b Madan Lal	22
R. J. Hadlee	b Abid Ali	15
D. R. Hadlee	not out	8
Extras (b 8, lb 5)		13

Total (6 wkts) 233

Overs: 58.5.

Did not bat: B. J. McKechnie, H. J. Howarth, R. O. Collinge.

Fall of wickets: 1-45, 2-63, 3-70, 4-135, 5-185, 6-224.

Bowling: Madan Lal 11.5-1-62-1, Amarnath 8-1-40-1, Bedi 12-6-28-1, Abid Ali 12-2-35-2, Venkat 12-0-39-0, Solkar 3-0-16-0.

New Zealand won by 4 wickets.

Umpires: W. L. Budd, A. E. Fagg.

Man of the Match: G. M. Turner.

Adjudicator: J. B. Statham.

This was a match full of fluctuations and uncertainties which underlined the toughness of the Prudential competition as well as its glamour. Cocktail parties can be fun, meetings with old friends warm and nostalgic, but when the pads are on and the bat is swinging it is simply a matter of death to one or the other in the space of a day.

So it was for India at Old Trafford, but it required a truly outstanding innings from Glenn Turner to swing it New Zealand's way, and there were just seven balls left in the contest when they achieved their target.

Glenn Turner is interesting on the subject of one-day cricket, the game which many believe is the wrong grounding for a young batsman. With overs expiring there is less and less time to settle in at the crease, over-ambitious shots are attempted before the eye and the feet are in accord, and bad habits form quickly. Turner on the other hand, believes that the shorter game has widened the scope of his own play, forced him to look for his strokes and brought him a fluency of run-getting which he once did not possess. Certainly he was a defensively-minded player when he came to Worcestershire from New Zealand and I would not dispute his conviction for a moment. His advantage is that he opens the batting. There is time to defend for a while before releasing the more ambitious shots. The harm is done to those lower down the order who are trying to learn the game with a heave and a slog.

Turner's was one of two worthwhile innings in this match, the other came low down in the Indian batting order from Abid Ali. When Abid appeared at the crease India were 94 for 5. Gaekwad alone had threatened to occupy the 'middle' long enough to build an innings, though this only by the courtesy of Wadsworth, who put down a straightforward catch behind the wicket.

Mixing orthodox cover driving of classic correctness with good old-fashioned, uninhibited slogging, Abid moved to his half century with a six, crisply struck off Collinge, over mid-wicket. He scurried between the wickets, upset the New Zealanders' field placings and loosened their grip on the game. His captain Venkat was moved to play some fine shots himself, Bedi managed to thump a four and the total of 230, although not large enough to make them favourites, was certainly something to bowl at, and much depended on the luck of Turner, the only New Zealand batsman likely to dominate a whole innings. Yet this he did, his undefeated century occupying 163 minutes and containing twelve fours. 'Turner rides Ali's punch' read the *Sunday Telegraph* headline.

There was a period of tight Indian bowling and fielding but Turner was immovable. He had scored 171 not out in the first match of this series, 12 against England and this time 114 not out, these adding up to 297 runs for only once out. Morrison, his partner, did not get off the mark until the sixth over, falling to Bedi's second delivery, caught down the leg side by Engineer. This was unlucky enough for the batsman but poor Howarth had the even worse frustration of seeing Abid Ali deflect the ball on to the bowler's wicket when stretching over to stop Turner's fierce drive so that he was run out.

Turner combined that solid upright defensive lunge forward with sumptuous stroke-play, though he lost his Worcestershire colleague Parker, lbw, just before tea. Bedi bowled superbly, giving strength to the argument that a good bowler is always a good bowler under any circumstances. His twelve overs cost only 28 runs and he took one wicket. It was Hastings who eventually dropped an anchor with Turner. Wadsworth and Richard Hadlee too chipped in strongly and victory was theirs with an over to go, though it could have been advanced a little if the pressure had been on them. Pressures will certainly be on them on Saturday when they meet the West Indies in the semi-final.

THE OVAL; Saturday, June 14th, 1975

Group B: West Indies beat Australia by 7 wickets

AUSTRALIA		
R. B. McCosker	c Fredericks, b Julien	0
A. Turner	lbw, b Roberts	7
I. M. Chappell	c Murray, b Boyce	25

G. S. Chappell	c Murray, b Boyce	15
K. D. Walters	run out	7
R. Edwards	b Richards	58
R. W. Marsh	not out	52
M. H. N. Walker	lbw, b Holder	8
J. R. Thomson	c Holder, b Richards	1
D. K. Lillee	b Roberts	3
A. A. Mallett	c Murray, b Roberts	0
Extras (lb 9, w 1, nb 6)		16
	Total	192

Overs: 53.4.
Fall of wickets: 1-0, 2-21, 3-49, 4-56, 5-61, 6-160, 7-173, 8-174, 9-192.
Bowling: Julien 12-2-31-1, Roberts 10.4-1-39-3, Boyce 11-0-38-2, Holder 10-0-31-1, Lloyd 4-0-19-0, Richards 6-0-18-2.

WEST INDIES

R. C. Fredericks	c Marsh, b Mallett	58
C. G. Greenidge	lbw, b Walker	16
A. I. Kallicharran	c Mallett, b Lillee	78
I. V. A. Richards	not out	15
R. B. Kanhai	not out	18
Extras (lb 2, b 4, w 3, nb 1)		10
	Total (3 wkts)	195

Overs: 46.
Did not bat: C. H. Lloyd, B. D. Julien, D. L. Murray, K. D. Boyce, V. A. Holder, A. M. E. Roberts.
Fall of wickets: 1-29, 2-153, 3-159.
Bowling: Lillee 10-0-66-1, Thomson 6-1-21-0, Walker 12-2-41-1, G. S. Chappell 4-0-13-0, Mallett 11-2-35-1, I. M. Chappell 3-1-9-0.
West Indies won by 7 wickets.
Umpires: H. D. Bird, D. J. Constant.
Man of the Match: A. I. Kallicharran.
Adjudicator: L. E. G. Ames.

I had fears about a lack of tension in this game which were unfounded. Both sides were assured of a semi-final place. Would this therefore be reason for players to relax a little? Would they keep the long knives in the sheaths for another and more vital day?

If there were inclinations that way in the hearts of the

players themselves as they made their way to the Oval by coach on a hot summer's morning, they would have been dispelled by the sights and sounds at the Hobbs Gates. The atmosphere smelled unmistakably of war. Ticket touts assured me in their Caribbean best that I could watch the best side in the world cut down their challengers for a mere £10. The price was forbidding to most and so the many West Indians who could not burst past the gatemen with a wide smile and a fiver, had to resort to cat-burglar methods. Walls were scaled and coloured children dropped over like leaves from trees. It was rumoured that those with tickets pretended to be pushed from behind past the poor gatemen so that they did not have to hand over their counterfoils. Then after downing a hasty beer they would pop the ticket into the beer can and lob it back high over the wall to waiting accomplices. A large dray carrying beer barrels entered the pavilion car-park with official sanction. Out from behind the barrels leapt a dozen young men like something out of Ali Baba and the Forty Thieves.

The atmosphere inside the ground defied the players producing anything but an authentic battle and in this summer of extraordinary sunshine, the heavens were blue and beautiful.

And so it was, on such a day, that the West Indies committed an act of destruction so violent, yet so brilliantly flamboyant as only they can, to pass Australia's score of 192, losing just 3 wickets, and this by the 46th over. Little Alvin Kallicharan was declared Man of the Match as a parade of his countrymen danced back and forth in front of the pavilion clanging away at their improvised steel band—whistles, beer cans and an old wooden box. A policeman nodded with a patient smile as an overjoyed supporter wound his arms about him, yelling an inch away from his face 'Andy Pandy make Thomson into spinner'. Yet the Roberts, Thomson, Lillee confrontation was just one aspect of a match which will be long remembered. The 'tom-toms' beat in Kennington long after the sun had gone down.

From the moment that West Indian captain Clive Lloyd won the toss and asked Australia to bat they looked unstoppable. Roy Fredericks quickly picked up a catch to dismiss McCosker at leg slip off the left-arm inswing of Bernard Julien, and Roberts, gunsmoke in his nostrils, beat Turner and Ian Chappell for pace on a wicket which was clearly on the slow side. In response to the chant 'Bowl 'im kid', Andy Roberts struck Turner such a blow just under the knee of the back leg that he almost cut him in half. The verdict was lbw and the score 21 for 2.

The Chappell brothers came together and impressed their determination and techniques on the situation. They directed the ball strongly through the mid-wicket area and were prepared to drop the lifting delivery at their toes with a straight bat. Importantly they saw off Roberts who was withdrawn from the attack after six overs, conceding just 10 runs. Julien's control was faultless, too—9 overs, 1 for 20.

If Clive Lloyd had a problem at this stage it centred on the make-up of his attack which, as at Edgbaston against Pakistan, lacked Lance Gibbs. Yet difficulties never arose because Lloyd himself sent down four overs, while Richards again surprised everyone by taking 2 wickets for 18 runs in 6 overs. These two did not follow Roberts. This job was entrusted to Holder and Boyce who expertly pushed on the process of winkling out the Australian batsmen. The most spectacular dismissal was that of Walters. He had been testing the fielders from the start, eager to keep the score ticking along. He took a cheeky run to Fredericks in the gully and many quick singles in that favourite corner of all Aussies, mid-wicket. Patrolling this territory was Gordon Greenidge, removed from the slip area because he had a painful back.

Walters once again probed the space between mid-on

and mid-wicket, Greenidge ran to his left, picking up the ball in his left hand, transferring to his right and almost in one gesture threw down the stumps at the bowler's end, Walters groping in vain for the crease. It was a harsh ending to a great day for the batsman because that morning the announcement was made of the Queen's award of the MBE for his services to Australian cricket.

The West Indian chatter around the ground at lunch-time, Australia 76 for 5, was loud and cocksure. Refreshment stalls had loaded up especially with pineapple, watermelon and mango. 'Put in a peach for me. I pick it off de tree' some wandering minstrel teased the young girl who served him. The fruiterer probably made one mistake; the sale of his Cape oranges was rather slow to say the least! Some found their enjoyment by getting to the bottom of a bottle of Vodka, but no one offended. It was a fun day, the early skirmish had left Australia with a bloody nose, and no West Indian was going to pass off a chance like that for making merry.

In the Long Room where life was quieter, the former England wicket keeper, Godfrey Evans, sat 'in state' at the Ladbroke's table weighing up odds to be offered at the betting tent. He is Ladbroke's adviser. The West Indian money had been flooding on all day and he wore a look of concern as he lengthened the odds against Australia.

The 25,000 spectators settled again after the interval as Edwards and Marsh, fighters both, attempted to re-assemble the innings. They both managed to put away the bad ball and tucked the good ones cleverly behind square on the leg side. Edwards eventually realised the truth of the situation. Richards was the bowler, the faster men were due back; he had to make his move against the off-spin rather than wait. He leapt at Richards, cracked him for a couple of fours, refused to acknowledge the warning lights and was bowled attempting to repeat the performance.

(above) 'The battle is o'er'—West Indies take the first Prudential Cup at Lord's

Flashback to 1973 for the sight that never was in 1975. Geoff Boycott in an England sweater

Surrey members at The Oval say goodbye to Colin Cowdrey in September

No gloves have ever claimed more victims. 1975 was the end of the road for John Murray of Middlesex and England

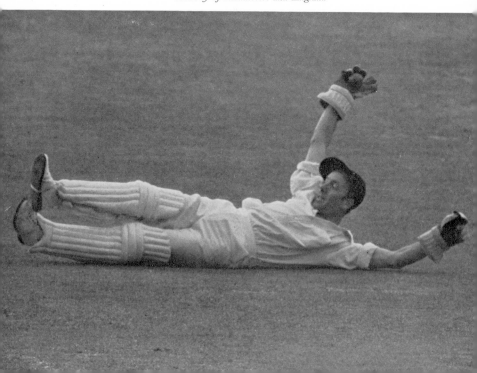

They had put on 99 for the 6th wicket but the return of Roberts was enough to see off the tail.

Indeed one of the special roars of the day was reserved for Roberts as he raced in to bowl at Jeff Thomson. Thomson was hit on the forearm. It hurt. He swished the bat and missed and tried all the well-known gestures to make the crowd laugh. They were not amused. Supporters of England had suffered a winter of frustration as Thomson had torn into our batsmen and intimidated them in Australia. They wanted his blood and the West Indians were happy that their fast man should prove that he, not Thomson, was the fastest in the world. 'Andy Roberts. Faster than any kangaroo' was one banner waved at this very moment. Thomson departed lamely, skying a catch off Richards, but satisfaction may have been achieved when Roberts uprooted Dennis Lillee's stumps. 192 all out and the West Indies openers could be sure that the pace and the bouncers would be reciprocated.

It was certainly tough for Fredericks and Greenidge. Both were not at their best before the game. Fredericks, as mentioned before, was the only member of his side not engaged in English cricket, therefore it was out-of-season for him. Greenidge was having no luck with Hampshire and suffering a noticeable lack of confidence. Yet they saw off Dennis Lillee and Jeff Thomson at their fastest (though I would guess that Thomson's rhythm is far from right). Fredericks hooked both of them, the gauntlet was down, there was to be no ducking and diving from the bouncers.

As Fredericks attacked more and more, that tiny Guyanan Alvin Kallicharan, 5 ft. 4 in., dapper and left-handed, proceeded to play a genuinely rhapsodic innings, sometimes lissom, often brutal. He took on Lillee in a cavalier but resolute way, not sitting on the splice with teeth clenched and muscles taut, just relaxed aggression. The more Lillee dropped short, the further he hooked

C

him or cut him. When the ball was pitched up outside the off-stump he sent drives screaming through the covers, full-length half volleys hit off the back foot in true West Indian fashion. The Australians bowled with their usual hostility but if there was a fault it was that they tended to pitch too short. Ian Chappell too has something to learn in the art of defensive cricket, though, knowing his style as I do, I suspect he has no great regard for defensive strategies. In full flow, Kallicharan despatched Lillee with a crack of the bat to many parts of the field. One sequence of ten balls went thus—4, 4, 4, 4, 4, 1, 4, 6, 0, 4.

However, far from being a guide to the outcome of the Prudential competition, Australia must nurse their moral wounds in the knowledge that the West Indies are as likely to do this to a great side as they are to miss out against a side with nowhere near their own talent and flair. All that was resolved on this memorable day's sport at the Oval was that Australia were to face the harder of the two semi-finals, England at Headingley. New Zealand must then stir up something above the ordinary to prevent West Indies being at Lord's for the final.

EDGBASTON; Saturday, June 14th, 1975

Group A: England beat East Africa by 196 runs

ENGLAND		
B. Wood	b Quaraishy	77
D. L. Amiss	c Nana, b Zulfiqar	88
F. C. Hayes	b Zulfiqar	52
A. W. Greig	lbw, b Zulfiqar	9
A. P. E. Knott	not out	18
C. M. Old	b Quaraishy	18
M. H. Denness	not out	12
Extras (b 7, lb 7, w 1, nb 1)		16
Total (5 wkts)		290

Innings closed.
Did not bat: K. W. R. Fletcher, J. A. Snow, P. Lever, D. L. Underwood.
Fall of wickets: 1-158, 2-192, 3-234, 4-244, 5-277.
Bowling: Frasat Ali 9-0-40-0, Pringle 12-0-41-0, Nana 12-2-46-0, Sethi 5-0-29-0, Zulfiqar 12-0-63-3, Quraishy 10-0-55-2.

EAST AFRICA

Frasat Ali	b Snow	o
Sam Walusimba	lbw, b Snow	7
Yunus Badat	b Snow	o
Jawahir Shah	lbw, b Snow	4
Ramesh Sethi	b Lever	30
Harilal R. Shah	b Greig	6
Mehmood Quaraishy	b Greig	19
Zulfiqar Ali	b Lever	7
H. McLeod	b Lever	o
P. G. Nana	not out	8
D. Pringle	b Old	3
Extras (lb 6, w 1, nb 3)		10
	Total	94

Overs: 52.3.
Fall of wickets: 1-7, 2-7, 3-15, 4-21, 5-42, 6-72, 7-76, 8-79, 9-88.
Bowling: Snow 12-6-11-4, Lever 12-3-32-3, Underwood 10-5-11-0, Wood 7-3-10-0, Greig 10-1-18-2, Old 1.3-0-2-1.
England won by 196 runs.
Umpires: J. G. Langridge, W. E. Alley.
Man of the Match: J. A. Snow.
Adjudicator: R. T. Spooner.

England swamped East Africa in what turned out to be an academic exercise. East Africa put England in to bat in order to make the game last. Wood was brought in to replace Jameson, an indication perhaps that he is being viewed carefully with the Test series in mind later in the season.

This was not much of a test. Wood and Amiss put on 158 for the first wicket and that must have been enough to dampen the keenness of tougher campaigners like Knott and Greig. The crowd did voice their suspicion that England were sparing the rod to avoid unnecessary humiliation in the sunshine.

Glimpses of fallibility were shown by Amiss who, at 31, almost dropped a ball from Pringle on to his wicket and, at 56, he saw Nana, left arm slow, drop a shoulder high return catch. Yet Amiss was first to his fifty and first out at 88, giving a catch to mid-wicket on the last ball before lunch. Hayes was promoted in the order (Fletcher not being in need of the batting practice) and he played a gem of an innings. He lost Wood who was hitting across the line, attempting to force the pace, but continued to play some magnificent shots. He gently stroked the ball to the off-side boundary as well as hitting two sixes straight into the pavilion. Greig, of whom so much is expected, cannot get going with the bat. Probably he has played too much Test match cricket over the last few years, the smaller occasions lure him to the pitfalls of inconsistent concentration. There is no danger of his run-shortage lasting; he is far too correct a player for that.

East Africa's innings lay in ruins within a few overs, shattered by the one man who showed no appetite for dalliance, John Snow . . . 4 wickets for 11 runs in 12 overs. He was made Man of the Match. Yet East Africa gleaned as much experience as possible. Their modest 94 took them 53 overs. Sethi lasted 32 overs for 30 but otherwise there was a procession of flimsy techniques against fast bowling. Snow took the first four wickets for 5 runs.

Amateur cricketers always find the extra speed of professional fast bowling too much for them, though Snow is nothing like as speedy as he was.

It is even more of a test when the contest requires quick scoring. One can possibly get away with desperate shots against spin, but never against the faster men.

The East Africans have had an uncomfortable time of it and take their leave of the competition without having left a suggestion in the eyes of the British public that they will learn from the experience. There will be other countries asking for recognition next time, and I must be excused the bias of my homeland when I say that Wales, with its many Glamorgan county professionals available, would have presented a challenge much stronger than this. Why not Holland or Argentina too?

TRENT BRIDGE; Saturday, June 14th, 1975

Group B: Pakistan beat Sri Lanka by 192 runs

PAKISTAN

Sadiq Mohammad	c Opatha, b Warnapura	74
Majid Khan	c Tennekoon, b S. De Silva	84
Zaheer Abbas	b Opatha	97
Mushtaq Mohammad	c Heyn, b Warnapura	26
Wasim Raja	c Opatha, b Warnapura	2
Javed Miandad	not out	28
Imran Khan	b Opatha	0
Pervez Mir	not out	4
Extras (b 4, lb 4, w 2, nb 5)		15
	Total (6 wkts)	330

Innings closed.
Did not bat: Wasim Bari, Asif Masood, Naseer Malik.
Fall of wickets: 1-159, 2-168, 3-256, 4-268, 5-318, 6-318.
Bowling: Opatha 12-0-67-2, Pieris 9-0-54-0, A. De Silva 7-1-46-0, S. De Silva 12-1-61-1, Kaluperuma 9-1-35-0, Warnapura 8-0-42-3, Ransinghe 3-0-10-0.

SRI LANKA

R. Fernando	c & b Miandad	21
B. Warnapura	b Imran	2
A. Tennekoon	lbw, b Asif	30
M. Tissera	c Bari, b Sadiq	12
D. Heyn	c Zaheer, b Miandad	1
A. Ranasinghe	b Raja	9
M. Pieris	lbw, b Pervez	16
A. Opatha	c Zaheer, b Sadiq	0
S. De Silva	b Imran	26
L. Kaluperuma	not out	13

A. De Silva   c Raja, b Imran   o
    Extras (lb 1, w 3, nb 4)   8

                          Total   138

Overs: 50.1.

Fall of wickets: 1-5, 2-44, 3-60, 4-61, 5-75, 6-79, 7-90, 8-113, 9-135.

Bowling: Masood 6-2-14-0, Imran 7.1-3-15-3, Miandad 7-2-22-2, Malik 6-1-19-1, Sadiq 6-1-20-2, Raja 7-4-7-1, Mushtaq 5-0-16-0, Pervez 6-1-17-1.

Pakistan won by 192 runs.

Umpires: A. Jepson, T. W. Spencer.

Man of the Match: Zaheer Abbas.

Adjudicator: W. Voce.

Those present at this game said that they felt a sadness for Pakistan. They had been narrowly defeated by Australia and robbed by the Gods of victory over the West Indies in the toughest group in which only Sri Lanka could be considered inferior competitors. Their splendid stroke makers would be missed when next week's stage is set for the final acts.

So be it, but think therefore what a trial of skills this competition has been for Sri Lanka. Their moment of achievement came against Australia when they got within 52 of a score of 328, in the face of two of the fastest bowlers in the world.

In this match Pakistan were asked to bat by Tennekoon and they quickly exploded a barrage of brilliant shots, Majid and Sadiq opening with a partnership of 158 in 32 overs. Zaheer was to follow with 97 in 27 overs, looking set for a century when he played the ball down on to his wicket. Though not exuding quite the same panache as Majid, Zaheer was awarded the Man of the Match prize by the old England bowler Bill Voce. At 256 for 3 it was not surprising that Pakistan became a little careless, though after the 60 overs it was only by 4 runs that they failed to beat the one-day record of 334 made by England against India at Lord's a week ago.

Opatha was the liveliest of the seam attack, Kaluperuma the off-spinner was tidy, and S. de Silva lured Majid into holing out at long on.

When Sri Lanka went out to bat Ladbroke's were offering 500–1 against Sri Lanka scoring the 331 required to win. Fernando and Warnapura were brave without judgement, went for their shots in an all-out effort to win, but lost their wickets in doing so. It was an honest but hopeless performance.

The Pakistan leg-spinners caused most problems and rushed the match to its early conclusion. The seventeen-year-old Miandad caught and bowled Fernando, and then had David Heyn taken in the cover regions. Sadiq too was getting among the wickets. Soon Sri Lanka were 79 for 6. De Silva and Kaluperuma gave the withering tail a small flourish and eventually they managed to scramble 138. Tissera and Tennekoon did threaten to play major innings and both are good enough players. Tennekoon was dismissed by Naseer Malik in the classic manner, first the bumper which was signalled a 'wide' and then the yorker which trapped him lbw.

Note: It was decided at the International Cricket Conference's annual meeting at Lord's on June 25th and 26th that Sri Lanka's application for full membership should be left in abeyance for a further year, though given 'sympathetic' consideration.

So the tables at the close of the preliminary rounds stand as follows:

Group A	P	W	L	Pts
England	3	3	0	12
New Zealand	3	2	1	8
India	3	1	2	4
East Africa	3	0	3	0

Group B	P	W	L	Pts
West Indies	3	3	0	12
Australia	3	2	1	8
Pakistan	3	1	2	4
Sri Lanka	3	0	3	0

4 *Semi-finals*

HEADINGLEY; Wednesday, June 18th, 1975

Australia beat England by 4 wickets

ENGLAND

D. L. Amiss	lbw, b Gilmour	2
B. Wood	b Gilmour	6
K. W. R. Fletcher	lbw, b Gilmour	8
A. W. Greig	c Marsh, b Gilmour	7
F. C. Hayes	lbw, b Gilmour	4
M. H. Denness	b Walker	27
A. P. E. Knott	lbw, b Gilmour	o
C. M. Old	c G. S. Chappell, b Walker	o
J. A. Snow	c Marsh, b Lillee	2
G. G. Arnold	not out	18
P. Lever	lbw, b Walker	5
Extras (lb 5, w 7, nb 2)		14
	Total	93

Overs: 36.2.
Fall of wickets: 1-2, 2-11, 3-26, 4-33, 5-35, 6-36, 7-37, 8-52, 9-73.
Bowling: Lillee 9-3-26-1, Gilmour 12-6-14-6, Walker 9.2-3-22-3, Thomson 6-0-17-0.

AUSTRALIA

A. Turner	lbw, b Arnold	7
R. B. McCosker	b Old	15
I. M. Chappell	lbw, b Snow	2
G. S. Chappell	lbw, b Snow	4
K. D. Walters	not out	20
R. Edwards	b Old	o
R. W. Marsh	b Old	5
G. J. Gilmour	not out	28
Extras (b 1, lb 6, nb 6)		13
	Total (6 wkts)	94

Overs: 28.4.
Did not bat: M. H. N. Walker, D. K. Lillee, J. R. Thomson.
Fall of wickets: 1-17, 2-24, 3-32, 4-32, 5-32, 6-39.
Bowling: Arnold 7.4-2-15-1, Snow 12-0-30-2, Old 7-2-29-3, Lever 2-0-7-0.

Australia won by 4 wickets.
Umpires: W. E. Alley, D. J. Constant.
Man of the Match: G. J. Gilmour.
Adjudicator: J. B. Stollmeyer.

The mere sight of Ian Chappell's side recalled the nightmares of English batsmen in Australia during the winter, 'horror films' as viewed by cricket lovers on television screens in Britain. Now they were about to grapple again, though the prizes for success—a place in the final—and a large slice of the financial booty mattered less in everyone's mind than the restoration of national honour. Kallicharan and the West Indians had shown how Lillee and Thomson could be made to struggle on slow wickets, even Sri Lanka had got runs against them. Could England now lock the old skeletons away in the cupboard?

There were some fresh minds on the job. Barry Wood was to open the innings with Dennis Amiss, Frank Hayes was in at number 5 and John Snow, himself the scourge of Australians on the tour out there in 1971-2, was bowling well enough to test the memories of those who found him unpleasant to face three years previously. Yet talk of new faces ought not to exclude Australia's selection of left-arm fast-medium bowler Gary Gilmour.

The pitch was green, clouds had moved over the ground to displace the early morning sunshine, and as Mike Denness chose to leave out Derek Underwood and put a battery of seam bowling on to the field, so Ian Chappell omitted Ashley Mallett for Gilmour. No one could have imagined what impact that last move was to have on this game, one of the most extraordinary matches ever played between the two countries.

Chappell won the toss and sent England in to bat. He gave the new ball to Gilmour. Immediately Amiss was in trouble, the ball obviously swinging late. With the first ball of Gilmour's second over Amiss went, lbw. With the first ball of Gilmour's fourth and seventh overs respectively, Wood was yorked, and Greig induced to drive at a wide one, which had him magnificently caught right-handed by Marsh. Hayes drove Gilmour past mid-on for four, but then met a prodigious inswinger which had him lbw without playing a stroke. Fletcher grafted hard for an hour, yet had only 8 runs to show when he too fell, lbw to the first ball of Gilmour's ninth over. Knott went to the last ball of that over and the destruction was virtually complete. The ghosts walked again; bad dreams crowded in.

Alan Knott told me later that the ball had been terribly difficult to pick up from the bowler's hand. Sight screens on the boundary were positioned perfectly for the right arm over-the-wicket styles but not for Gilmour's left-arm over variety. The screens were apparently immovable.

Mike Denness settled in without much trouble but at the other end Old, on the back foot, was caught at second slip and Snow taken on the leg side off Lillee. Arnold played unexpectedly well but the worst had happened. Utter rout had been suffered; another humiliation in conditions which should theoretically have favoured England. Could anything be salvaged?

For a few minutes, around four o'clock, Headingley was living up to its reputation as the place where something is always likely to happen. One can recall the record of Sir Donald Bradman who faced England four times at Headingley, scoring 334 in 1930, 304 in 1934, 103 and 16 in 1938 and 33 and 173 not out in 1948! Not many seasons behind us either is the notorious pitch which afterwards proved to be afflicted with fuserium disease, and on which Underwood bowled out Australia in 1972. Now, in response to England's 93 in this Prudential Cup Semi-final, Australia were 39 for 6. Old and Snow had done the damage and something quite unbelievable seemed about to happen. The crowd were struck with a silent, crazy optimism.

The conditions had not changed much when Australia went in to bat, the clouds still floated across on a sharp cross-wind, and Turner and McCosker picked up 17 runs off Arnold and Snow. Turner was soon out lbw playing across the line and with just six runs between them the Chappell brothers were both lbw to Snow.

Snow had begun unsteadily—he was no-balled seven times and warned for running on the pitch—but he got better and better as Old put England right back into the game at the other end by bowling out McCosker, Edwards and Marsh in eight balls. It was a game without reason. How can you possibly win a 60-over match with a total of 93?

The answer is of course that you cannot. It takes too few lucky blows by the batting side to accumulate runs. For example Walters came to the crease and Denness, as is the practice of all captains, placed two gullies in preparation for a Walters weakness outside the off stump. Third slip moved squarer for the job. Needless to say, when Walters had made only 1, he sliced the ball into the gap just vacated.

Walters hung on but it was Gilmour who put bat to ball in the most positive way to make the game safe. Twice he drove Old past mid-off. He did edge Lever through the hands of Greig at second slip when the score was 78 and he was on 24, but victory was virtually safe by then and it had been very much his day.

He was, of course, Man of the Match and it would be wrong to infer that his achievements were all that lucky. He kept a full length and swung the ball both ways, and this at a lively pace. Obviously he puts one in mind of Alan Davidson. He wastes no time in extra steps before his bustling 12-stride run-up. He has played only three Tests and those against New Zealand. In his first match for New South Wales he made 104—believed to be the only player to signal his arrival on the first-class scene with a century between lunch and tea. English bowlers felt a touch of it in his 59 not out for New South Wales last November. Now just 23 years old, he was spotted by Sir Gary Sobers when he played in a Northern NSW XI six years ago.

So, in this flurry of action, England were bundled out of the Cup. In a way some prestige was recovered in the field but the blight still consumes the batting. It will be interesting to see if the selectors choose fresh minds to take on the Test series which starts shortly.

The Headingley pitch was criticised by Mike Denness, the England captain. 'I feel it is most unfortunate the match was played on the same strip used for the Australia *v* Pakistan game ten days ago,' he said.

'For such an important match we should have had a pitch on which the batsmen could play their shots. But the bounce was uneven, mostly on the low side, as you can tell from the number of lbw decisions.

'I understand the pitch had not been watered since the last game, and the grass allowed to grow.' Describing the game he commented 'Gilmour not only made the ball swing, but it was hitting the seam and coming back. I feel winning the toss was very important.'

Ian Chappell, the Australian captain, was perhaps naturally less scathing. 'The ball seamed all day and the bounce was uneven,' he said. 'It was difficult to get on the front foot against bowlers of pace. But perhaps it was a good thing batsmen did not have it all their own way.'

George Cawthray, the groundsman responsible for the pitch retaliated: 'The atmosphere decided which way the pitch played. It would have been the same if I had prepared another one.'

That just about sums up the bitter disappointment for England and the triumph for Australia. If anything it strengthens Australia's hand for the Test matches because Gary Gilmour could easily challenge the established trio—Thomson, Lillee and Walker. England are still vulnerable to faster bowling, albeit the swinging variety this time, though perhaps one can hold out hope for the return of John Snow, 33, who will not be anything like as fast as he used to be but who knows his trade well enough to use conditions like these at Headingley which favour the ball which hits the seam.

At the other end of the country, New Zealand were making their challenge to topple the West Indians before another excited crowd.

THE OVAL; Wednesday, June 18th, 1975

West Indies beat New Zealand by 5 wickets

NEW ZEALAND

G. M. Turner	c Kanhai, b Roberts	36
J. F. M. Morrison	lbw, b Julien	5
G. P. Howarth	c Murray, b Roberts	51
J. M. Parker	b Lloyd	3
B. F. Hastings	not out	24
K. J. Wadsworth	c Lloyd, b Julien	11
B. J. McKechnie	lbw, b Julien	1
D. R. Hadlee	c Holder, b Julien	0
B. L. Cairns	b Holder	10
H. J. Howarth	b Holder	0
R. O. Collinge	b Holder	2
Extras (b 1, lb 5, w 2, nb 7)		15
	Total	158

Overs: 52.2.

Fall of wickets: 1-8, 2-98, 3-105, 4-106, 5-125, 6-133, 7-139, 8-155, 9-155.

Bowling: Julien 12-5-27-4, Roberts 11-3-18-2, Holder 8.2-0-30-3, Boyce 9-0-31-0, Lloyd 12-1-37-1.

WEST INDIES

R. C. Fredericks	c Hastings, b Hadlee	6
C. G. Greenidge	lbw, b Collinge	55
A. I. Kallicharran	c & b Collinge	72
I. V. A. Richards	lbw, b Collinge	5
R. B. Kanhai	not out	12
C. H. Lloyd	c Hastings, b McKechnie	3

B. D. Julien   not out   4
    Extras (lb 1, nb 1)   2
                                                                 ──
                                       Total (5 wkts)   159
Overs: 40.1.
Did not bat: D. L. Murray, K. D. Boyce, V. A. Holder,
A. M. E. Roberts.
Fall of wickets: 1-8, 2-133, 3-139, 4-142, 5-151.
Bowling: Collinge 12-4-28-3, Hadlee 10-0-54-1, Cairns
6.1-2-23-0, McKechnie 8-0-37-1, H. J. Howarth 4-0-15-0.
West Indies won by 5 wickets.
Umpires: W. L. Budd, A. E. Fagg.
Man of the Match: A. I. Kallicharran.
Adjudicator: N. J. N. Hawke.

With great ease, but not without trying to take it too
easily at times, the West Indies overpowered New
Zealand. They reached their objective, 159, for the loss
of only 5 wickets in 40.1 overs. It was just enough of a
contest for them to sharpen their claws for the final on
Saturday.

They began their response with a few careless shots
and Fredericks was caught from a half-hearted hook at
square leg. However, a few overs of obvious concentration by Greenidge and Kallicharan laid the foundations
for yet another avalanche of Caribbean artistry—a second
wicket partnership of 125. The ball simply disappeared
to all parts of the ground, though the New Zealand
ground fielding was every bit as agile as the West Indians'
had been. The outfield itself, uncut since the Australian
game there four days ago, had looked slow in the
morning but with these two at the wicket the ball
positively leapt away—one, two or three bounces into
the crowd.

Kallicharan was the man in form and again the Man of
the Match as chosen by former Australian player Neil
Hawke. For some reason Hadlee was persuaded to test
Kallicharan with short deliveries on leg stump which the
tiny Guyanan lashed round in an arc between deep

square and fine leg. More important for the West Indies was the sight of Greenidge in his best belligerent form. The over-accentuated backward movement across the stumps which, in defence, has set him up as a perpetual lbw victim this season, had disappeared. He still was out lbw, but in attack this time. His stroke play was correct, though typically violent when calling on his big shots, the cover drive off the back foot and the pull over mid-wicket.

Clive Lloyd had earlier persisted with the theory of putting the opposition in to bat and though there was little in the atmosphere to suggest hidden tricks on a clear, sunny morning, Julien moved the ball around considerably, as his figures of 4 for 27 in 12 overs suggest. He varied his pace cleverly too, mixing hostile bouncers with full length, almost innocuous looking in-swingers. Morrison was quickly deceived, lbw on the back foot to a ball that moved in late off the seam.

Andy Roberts did not take a wicket in his first spell of six overs, but he certainly demonstrated that his appetite for war had not died. One short ball struck Morrison painfully on the shoulder and he tested the nerve of both Turner and Howarth.

These two New Zealanders—both familiar with the game in this country of course, Turner with Worcestershire and Howarth on his home Surrey ground—did most to establish a reasonable grip on the game. Howarth was sharp and impressive. He stood cool and upright, moved smartly into the drive or cut and profited from some wayward bowling down the leg side from Clive Lloyd. Then Turner suddenly expanded his ambitions. Some of his hooking of the fast bowling was perfectly executed, rolling his wrists and playing the ball safely downwards. Yet just after lunch his side began their decline from 92 for 1 to 106 for 4.

Turner went first, edging a ball from Roberts through the area of second slip where no one was standing. But

Edgbaston—The 1st Test: The time has arrived for Tony Greig to measure up the centre seat occupied for the last time by Mike Denness

(above) *The familiar agony abroad and at home. Amiss falls to Lillee, and England's prolific run-getter of 1974 is hustled out of Test cricket in 1975*

Jeff Thomson—not as happy facing the bouncer as bowling it!

Australia's whirly-bird, Max Walker

The Thomson spring, perfectly coiled

Kanhai hurled himself across from first slip, every inch of the leap belying the arrival of his fortieth birthday next Boxing Day. The important partnership, 90 runs in 23 overs, was broken and the New Zealand captain, who had scored two centuries in the Cup so far and won two Man of the Match awards, was gone.

Roberts tore in, inspired by the success, and next had Geoff Howarth nimbly caught low down behind the stumps. Thereafter followed some uncultured swings of the bat and some excellent bowling. Holder finished off the innings with three wickets, all bowled, but it was still Julien's variation which impressed most. He prompted mis-drives from Wadsworth and Hadlee, and trapped McKechnie lbw to complete his four wickets.

Hastings survived to the end by determination, and by ducking as bouncers flew over his head. Actually, he bent so low there was never a danger of his body being hit. But his bat, which he left pointing skywards like a periscope, appeared to be Roberts' favourite target.

Only big Dick Collinge had produced similar hostility for New Zealand. In his brisk left-arm over the wicket style he raised the odd spot of dust and got the occasional ball to dig in and lift. 3 wickets for 28 runs was his reward.

He removed Kallicharan with an excellent caught and bowled taking the ball as he fell forwards from a checked drive. Greenidge aimed to hook a ball not quite short enough and Richards quietly walked across an inswinger. The fall of these three West Indian wickets, in pursuit of 159, might have suited the West Indies if Clive Lloyd could have taken some practice. Only once has he batted in the competition and then briefly. However he left rather like Fredericks and Richards, to a casual stroke, flicking a full-length ball from McKechnie into the hands of Hastings at square leg. Even Julien toyed with the situation, lobbing up a catch between mid-on and mid-off which almost went to hand.

Maybe it takes the sternest possible challenge to extract maximum concentration from this highly talented West Indian side. Their rightful place is at Lord's in the final, and the clash of their flamboyance and Australian grit should make the perfect climax to a competition which cannot have gone better for players, spectators or the Pru' themselves.

5   *Prudential Cup Final*

LORD'S; Saturday, June 21st, 1975

West Indies beat Australia by 17 runs

WEST INDIES

R. C. Fredericks	hit wicket, b Lillee	7
C. G. Greenidge	c Marsh, b Thomson	13
A. I. Kallicharran	c Marsh, b Gilmour	12
R. B. Kanhai	b Gilmour	55
C. H. Lloyd	c Marsh, b Gilmour	102
I. V. A. Richards	b Gilmour	5
K. D. Boyce	c G. S. Chappell, b Thomson	34
B. D. Julien	not out	26
D. L. Murray	c & b Gilmour	14
V. A. Holder	not out	6
Extras (lb 6, nb 11)		17

Total (8 wkts)   291

Innings closed.
Did not bat: A. M. E. Roberts.
Fall of wickets: 1-12, 2-27, 3-50, 4-199, 5-206, 6-209, 7-261, 8-285.
Bowling: Lillee 12-1-55-1, Gilmour 12-2-48-5, Thomson 12-1-44-2, Walker 12-1-71-0, G. S. Chappell 7-0-33-0, Walters 5-0-23-0.

AUSTRALIA

A. Turner	run out	40
R. B. McCosker	c Kallicharran, b Boyce	7
I. M. Chappell	run out	62
G. S. Chappell	run out	15
K. D. Walters	b Lloyd	35
R. W. Marsh	b Boyce	11
R. Edwards	c Fredericks, b Boyce	28
G. J. Gilmour	c Kanhai, b Boyce	14
M. H. N. Walker	run out	7
J. R. Thomson	run out	21
D. K. Lillee	not out	16
Extras (b 2, lb 9, nb 7)		18

Total   274

Overs: 58.4.

Fall of wickets: 1-25, 2-81, 3-115, 4-162, 5-170, 6-195, 7-221, 8-231, 9-233.
Bowling: Julien 12-0-58-0, Roberts 11-1-45-0, Boyce 12-0-50-4, Holder 11.4-1-65-0, Lloyd 12-1-38-1.
West Indies won by 17 runs.
Umpires: H. D. Bird, T. W. Spencer.
Man of the Match: C. H. Lloyd.
Adjudicators: R. Benaud, K. F. Barrington, J. B. Stollmeyer.

All honour and glory to the West Indies! The fortnight's jamboree has ended with a royal handshake for Clive Lloyd, leader of the winning side, and the handing over of the Prudential Cup by HRH Prince Philip, the President of the MCC.

When struggles are tense between these two countries, it is often thought that the flint-hard cussedness of the Aussie outlasts the extravagance of the West Indian. But is that a fancy myth? Who will ever forget the glorious first Test at Brisbane in 1960–61, the popping-creases were alive with Australians diving in to snatch hectic singles to win the match in the final over. Four runs to win in four balls, Hall barges into Kanhai as he is about to catch Grout. Next ball Grout grovels in sweat and dust, run-out by the coolest possible throw from the boundary by Conrad Hunte. Two balls to go, one to win. Kline and Meckiff rush off for a quick single, Solomon swoops one handed and throws down one stump, the only one he could see, in a single movement. The famous tie, and the truth is that tense moments in cricket turn the legs of every human being to jelly from time to time.

So it was that Ian Chappell's Australia strained after the West Indian total of 291 on this hot summer's day. One minute they were calm, the next almost demented; many batsmen took quick singles which their partners had not agreed to take. Five of them were run-out!

As a final it was all one could ever have hoped for a brave new venture in sponsorship. Two hours before the start, spectators gushed out of the underground station at St. John's Wood, queues snaked right around the walls and cars filtered slowly into the park at the Nursery end. A capacity crowd and another hot shirt-sleeved day, completing the meteorological miracle which has blessed every single moment of this competition with blue skies and sunshine.

Ian Chappell won the toss for Australia and sent the opposition in to bat though there was nothing in the air that remotely sniffed of Headingley. Chappell had in mind, more likely, Lloyd's habit of 'inserting' others.

It had been West Indies' formula for victory all through the tournament so now, before a ball had been bowled in anger, perhaps Chappell had snatched away their good luck charm.

Gilmour, scourge of England, was no-balled three times in the first over, making it clear where the strongest West Indian encampment was. Bells rang out alongside the Tavern and flags were waved. The hubbub died down as Fredericks and Greenidge prepared to take on Dennis Lillee.

Fredericks is a compulsive hooker, sometimes a little chancy, especially with the shot that goes down to the fine-leg region. With typical West Indian lavishness he is happy to gamble, just to see the ball sail for six and will consider himself hard done-by if a fielder hangs on to a skier on the boundary fence. Well, this time he responded to Lillee's bouncer (one of the few in the match) with a mighty swing of the bat. The ball cleared the fielder this time; all eyes followed it, yet there was a trick to the eye which fooled almost everyone. As he spun around in the crease, Fredericks had lost his foothold and slipped against the stumps, dislodging both bails . . . hit wicket bowled Lillee 7. West Indies 12 for 1. There was a certain amount of bad luck in this dismissal for the batsman, and good fortune for the bowler. It was a well judged bouncer putting Fredericks under pressure but possibly the crucial factor was that Fredericks was wearing boots with rubber soles. Most professional players would not dream of going into a match which starts as early as eleven o'clock in the morning, when some moisture may still be retained in the turf, without spiked footwear.

To the hero's acclaim, out strode Kallicharan to face bowlers who could not have felt too happy about his treatment of them a week before at the Oval. His innings began with the confident ring of the bat, but perhaps he was lured into the trap of over-confidence. To a ball from Gilmour outside the off stump he tried a square cut, a flicked shot, feet out of position, the ball too close and bouncing reasonably high off a smooth slow surface. Marsh accepted the snick behind the wicket. 27 for 2 bringing Kanhai to the crease to join Greenidge.

They were now edging from a defensive corner and there was obvious unevenness of bounce which the height of Max Walker emphasised when he came on to bowl. Frequently he struck the splice of Kanhai's bat. Kanhai got well and truly stuck in a defensive rut and even lost Greenidge, caught low down by Marsh from a slower ball by Thomson.

Then Clive Lloyd loped into the arena wearing cap, spectacles and a quizzical look on his face. How often has he contradicted his studious appearance with thoughts of violence! Lillee was immediately brought back, but in easy, destructive style, the West Indies captain hooked a collosal six; then off the back foot, coaxed Walker through the cover field. To this point Ian Chappell had persevered with two slips and a gully, but the time had come to dream up defensive patterns. Men were despatched to deep positions on the mid-wicket and square-cover boundaries. Edwards dropped him at 26. Meanwhile at the other end, poor Kanhai limped on, eleven overs passing without his scoring a run. Experience told him that as long as Lloyd was plundering on he must persevere. The partnership realised 149 in 36 overs and this was the record stand for the whole competition.

Lloyd's hundred came in 82 balls, and if figures alone do not persuade the world that something very special was happening, the inhabitants of London NW8 will tell how the mere sound of his bat, hammering out the music sweet to West Indian ears, destroyed their afternoon sleep!

It was an innings of surpassing talent and power. When Lloyd is at the crease, mid-on and mid-off automatically withdraw ten yards or so. His defensive pushes roast the hands like a lesser man's drives. Although his back foot wanders involuntarily in a small circle as the faster bowlers rush at him, he quickly beds it down on or around middle-and-leg and then levers off it into his strong front-foot attack. There is no shot he cannot play but one or two are not played by any other with the same ease. At his most vicious he 'picked up' balls from Walker, just a fraction short of good length in line with the middle and leg stumps. These he flipped to square leg off the front foot, and sent the ball with a few bounces into the rails, just like sending a flat pebble hopping over a calm sea. Of course his long reach upsets the bowler's length. Without doubt he is one of the most dangerous batsmen in the world because he can change the drift of a match within such a short space of time. Ideal for one-day cricket, and it was yet another stroke of fortune for all who watched that he reserved this great innings for the final.

Gilmour eventually came back with a tight spell of bowling which swung the game marginally back Australia's way. He got rid of Kanhai, Lloyd and Richards—209 for 6 in the 46th over.

One sadness was that Lloyd's innings should end in argument and confusion. Marsh 'went up' with Gilmour for a catch down the leg side. Gilmour prolonged the appeal, stared expectantly at umpire Bird, even though the adjudicator had turned to stone; but then after conferring with umpire Spencer, Bird gave Lloyd out. Kanhai took off his hat for more than the heat; Lloyd left his verbal mark on the 'middle' and a few missiles entered the arena from the terraces.

However, Australia's grip was promptly cracked open. One of the more unpredictable West Indians decided that the moon was in his quarter that day, and straightway the bowlers felt the lash of Keith Boyce. Julien supported with Murray and when you think of it, the strength of batting is limitless when you have Deryck Murray, who has opened in Tests, lurking away at number nine. 291 for 8 was the total. To have beaten that would have set a record for the competition.

Just think how close Australia came! They began securely enough even though there is nothing in the styles of either Turner or McCosker to excite to aesthetes. McCosker particularly got turned round to work the ball through mid-wicket and when the score was 25 Boyce produced just the ball to penetrate. It swung away, found the outside edge of the bat and landed safely in the eager fingers of Kallicharan at second slip. It was low and beautifully caught. Turner's authority increased while Ian Chappell quickly showed that he was at his belligerent best. Then came the first of the run-outs. A complete misunderstanding left Turner racing for safety. Only a direct hit would beat him and that is exactly what Richards produced in underarm style.

The Chappell brothers then put on 34 with mounting certainty until the plague returned—Greg was run out. Ian ran the ball out square on the off side. Greenidge and Richards could not agree over who was to field it. Greenidge relaxed, Richards turned and recovered the ball, then on the pivot he threw down the only stump of three which he could possibly see. Luck was going with the West Indies.

The third run-out was beyond all comprehension, especially as it saw off the captain himself, and would you believe it, Richards again was the destroyer. He first fumbled the ball, persuading Australia to break the

PRUDENTIAL CUP FINAL 89

PRUDENTIAL CUP FINAL 89

golden rule 'Never run for a misfield', then spun around and fired the ball just above the bails like a rifle shot. Lloyd, the bowler, clipped off the bails.

Australia were well in with a chance before this latest casualty because Walters had settled in to play handsomely. Perhaps they misread the situation; the outfield was as fast as glass, they could well win. Or possibly they wanted to hustle before Roberts came back.

Whatever the causes the slide was started. Walker was the fourth man to be run-out and Thomson the fifth.

It is often agony at the end of the day to weigh up the mistakes. The turning points, camouflaged then, stand up and mock you. Will Ian Chappell recall his superb innings or the five run-outs when he remembers this day? His side required 130 runs off the last 22 overs—very possible in fine batting conditions; then 76 off 10 with 4 wickets standing. Gilmour skied, Edwards too, but the character of the side came through when Lillee and Thomson embarked on a last-wicket partnership of bravado, surprising judgement and humour too. They came in at 233 with 52.5 overs gone. Within minutes their cutting and carving had West Indian fielders perched on the boundaries conceding the singles. The score mounted; 21 wanted from 2 overs. It *was* possible, and even more so when Thomson struck a no-ball in the air to Fredericks at cover. Fredericks threw at the bowler's wicket for a run-out; no one backed up and Lillee and Thomson raced the overthrows. Suddenly the field was full of West Indian spectators who, not hearing the call for no-ball, believed Thomson caught and the match won. It was an incredible sight. Fielders were knocked flying in the avalanche, the ball disappeared altogether, but calmly in midfield Lillee and Thomson ran their runs. Could they run 21 off one ball if the ball was not returned?

'Dead ball' was called by the umpires, 3 runs given. Within a minute Thomson was properly out. He played and missed, the ball went through to Murray. Thomson believed Lillee was going to chance running to the wicket-keeper, but instead he was sent back, and it was a fitting summary of Australia's innings to see Murray throw down the wicket without any trouble at all, while Thomson lay covered in dust, a few inches out. This final gallop by the demon fast bowlers revealed that Australia knew how to lose with humour. A game which begins at 11 a.m. and ends at 8.42 p.m. inevitably kills and rekindles hopes by the minute and by the hour; it chars the nerve-ends, bringing, eventually, the delirium of victory for one and that unwelcome stoicism to the other. To the Australians' credit, they charged to their defeat with style and without a single bleat about one-day cricket not being to their liking. Yet as Ian Chappell confessed when asked to comment on the competition, 'Enough is enough'—and I am sure he was right. Meanwhile, none could deny the West Indians the right to wear the first Prudential crown, nor could there be any argument that their captain, Clive Lloyd, was the Man of this unique Match.

What about the players and the Pru'?

Before this season, in the minds of those who had to play it, international one-day cricket was always the necessary evil which followed the Test matches.

Players always welcome the extra money and set out to see that justice is done on the field for the sponsor's sake. There are other motivations too. Old rivalries die hard. Dennis Lillee, for example, is not going to take a pounding from Tony Greig, if he can help it, at any sport, Prudential or ping-pong. Large crowds help to build up the atmosphere. People enjoy the prospect of the best cricketers rushing at each other's throats in a duel to instant death, and so in a way, full theatres draw more out of the protagonists themselves.

Yet the actual contests before this competition have meant little more than that. There have been no tears, curses or recriminations in the losing dressing room. No one has sat, head in hands, limp with disbelief as he would if a Test Match had been lost. Prudential cricket results have mattered little.

This one had to be different if only because it was the very reason why eight countries found themselves in conflict at the same time. It was unique. It also came before the Tests; no side-show this time. The players laughed at the International Cricket Conference's special legislation aimed to defeat intimidatory fast bowling in the competition, so cooling the battle.

It was decided that a short-pitched ball which passed over the head of a batsman standing normally at the crease should be called a wide. Yet it was obvious that the ball that whistles overhead has never been the problem. It is the ball that rises from short of a length and arrives like lightning about a yard in front of your nose that brings down the red mist. That is intimidatory bowling. So when a batsman ducked under a short-pitched ball, the umpire had to judge whether or not it would have passed over his head if he was still upright. The legislation certainly made it a waste of time to dig in the big bouncer and also ensured that every ball could be reached, but on those dry, firm wickets, no captain was going to fail to release the hostility of Lillee, Thomson, Roberts, Boyce, Holder, Old, Lever, Asif Masood and others.

Going back to his mark, that much feared West Indian destroyer Charlie Griffiths was once being stirred up by a team-mate standing at mid-off. He whispered, 'Give 'im de throat ball Charlie' . . . and that one, I can promise you, does not pass sweetly over the top of your head. So, although bouncers were rare in the final, there were enough reminders given to batsmen during the fortnight that the ruling was no deterrent. Perhaps it just helped to keep tempers under control. It would not have done so in Test Matches.

Otherwise the cricket was played with maximum effort and next time, because one presumes there must be a next time, countries may be more anxious about the programme of practice matches, which will give them a chance to get their whole squad into top form.

So from all points of view it was a complete success. Grounds were almost always full, there was excitement which never spilled over into hooliganism; disappointment which was dispelled by the sportsmanship of the occasion. The exception was the Indian match at Lord's but that was soon forgotten.

The Prudential company have already declared their willingness to do it again. They must understand that it can never be as brilliant a success as this. The weather was unbeatable and the financial situation could scarcely be bettered. The Prudential, by their sponsorship of some £150,000 promotional expenditure, catering and prize money, and the BBC fee of £50,000, covered the expenses. of the operation. The profits of about £200,000 will be divided between England (10%) and the other competing countries (7½%) each. The remainder will go into a general fund.

A survey carried out by Gallup just before and after the final of the Prudential Cup showed that 57% of the men in Great Britain had followed these matches. The event appealed to many who normally take little interest in cricket and this I know has given the players who took part much satisfaction.

What of the future of the Cup? The countries of the International Cricket Conference went away to discuss it with their own Boards. India, with Pakistan's support, have suggested that they may be the hosts next time.

However England may well be thought the best venue again. Nowhere else is there such a large immigrant population on hand to support every nation. Nor are the grounds so closely situated. Furthermore the English season does not coincide with others, which means that many overseas players are already resident playing for their counties, or would find it easy to leave their own countries out of season.

Wherever, whenever . . . it will happen again that all the best players in the world, South Africans too perhaps, will meet to test each other in the short game.

Geoffrey Boycott has long been accepted as the best batsman in England. His techniques have been built up by a singlemindedness in pursuit of the craft which has taken him into net-practice after net-practice in all corners of the cricket world. On MCC tours, instead of asking about the sights, the profitable merchandise or the night life, Boycott will ask simply for good net wickets to be put at his disposal and as many bowlers who care to wear themselves out in sunshine or snow. He has played 65 Test matches for England between 1964 and 1974. Before this 1975 season he had scored 85 centuries. He is the only English player ever to average a hundred in a home season.

On May 24th he declared himself unavailable to represent England this summer, the important summer of World Cup and Ashes. Yet he will play for Yorkshire. His motives one minute appear simple and sound, then unsportingly selfish the next. He issued a statement through Lord's, taking care to do it before the England captaincy for the Prudential Cup matches was announced, because his open wish is to lead his country and he wanted to avoid the conclusion being reached that he had opted out once Mike Denness had been chosen. His poor regard for Denness, under whose captaincy he refused to tour last winter, clouds the argument further, but as far as this day in May is concerned, Boycott's refusal to wear an England sweater starts with the following statement:

'For the first time in eighteen months, I have

basically found peace and contentment in cricket. I am enjoying the game and do not want anything to upset the present trend.

'I regard my main task as that of leading Yorkshire back to supremacy and the next two summers are going to be important ones. There is more to cricket than batting all day and getting plenty of runs. Now I want to concentrate on developing the future of the game in Yorkshire where I believe I am best appreciated.'

Geoff Boycott's last Test match before this decision was against India, in the first home Test of the 1974 season. He withdrew from the remaining games, missed the subsequent series against Pakistan and then the winter tour in Australia. There was still a lingering hope that changes in the selection panel might restore his keenness to play. Ken Barrington, for example, spent a couple of hours talking over the issues with him. Charlie Elliot, an umpire whom Boycott would respect and Sir Len Hutton whose experience and skill is legend, were the others recently allied to the Chairman Alec Bedser. Was it Bedser or Denness, or both, who had raised the hackles?

Boycott's attitude was no surprise; he was simply perpetuating the stalemate which grew up principally out of Denness's succession to Illingworth as England's captain. This came about after the season of 1973 when first England struggled to beat New Zealand and then suffered a crushing defeat from the West Indies. Denness had been selected for none of these six Tests, yet was chosen to take the MCC side to the West Indies the following winter, when Illingworth was discarded. To Boycott this was a stinging slap in the face because he had been Illingworth's deputy.

However that winter Boycott soldiered dutifully under Denness, making no secret of his intolerance of the captain. There was not a glimmer of personal friendship to make the situation work. Denness had been thrust into the uneasy position of having to prove himself as a Test class batsman as well as a captain. Boycott not only felt personal grievance but also frustration that England were relegating themselves to mediocrity by weak decisions at the top.

Not many would subscribe to the captaincy being handed down to Boycott on the basis of seniority alone, or by the favour of a retiring captain, for Illingworth believed Boycott to be the right man. Had Boycott the personal qualities to attract the players' loyalty? His career has been riddled with tales of selfishness and conceit, two qualities which can upset teammates, or alternatively live under the roof of singlemindedness and not offend the more tolerant. It would depend on England players spotting the soft, sensitive side of Boycott, behind the front of strong self-opinion.

Back in 1962 when he was new to the game Boycott, the bespectacled civil servant, impressed everyone by his intent to master the art of batsmanship. Within two seasons he was in the England side. Over a period of ten years and 65 Tests he has been striding confidently through county grounds and clubhouses, never slow to project himself (whether he realised it or not) as an insatiable run-hunter; and the best player in the country. There was a splendid honesty in this, all the more so because he actually achieved what he set out to do. He was much admired.

Yet perfectionists get hurt and are notoriously hard on those around them, whose standards fall below theirs. Geoff Boycott became a super-player, with an agent to exploit commercial ventures, and a life far less private than was perhaps good for the sensitive young man from Fitzwilliam, in Yorkshire. In a way, his retreat to Yorkshire 'where I believe I am best appreciated', is rather like the scared monkey who retreats to the branches of the tree he loves best. (I would not expect this

Dennis Lillee—concentration, speed and the art of rhythmical movement

The tables are turned. Doug Walters prepares to fight off the hat-trick ball from Phillippe Edmonds at Headingley

point to be conceded by Geoff or his supporters.) There are other theories which to my mind are mistaken. He would not shirk the speed of Dennis Lillee and Jeff Thomson, though he missed ten Tests against them. He is vulnerable against the fastest bowling only by his own high standards of performance. His confidence certainly was not broken by the little Indian left-arm seam bowler, Eknath Solkar, though some suggested that at the time.

Since 1971, Boycott's Yorkshire captaincy has survived disputes with committeemen and with senior players. He was on the verge of losing the job in many people's eyes at the close of 1974. That he fought back almost exclusively with young players says much for his leadership. Only a few weeks before the end of this 1975 season Yorkshire were being tipped for the title.

Yet there remains one matter of principle which shatters the playing fraternity. To turn your back on your country is, in the eye of every first-class player in the world, the ultimate treachery. Just consider players in English counties who have spent a career on the fringe of honours, who value the crown and lions and regarded Boycott so highly because he had done magnificently in that sweater. These are the players who now ask whether Geoffrey Boycott should be allowed to play for Yorkshire at all when England have a game and he has refused selection. They would stir the Yorkshire committee too and ask them to consider their responsibility in the matter. Yorkshire accept their share of Test match revenue, they support England—yet their best player does not. Loud voices and arguments echo around the committee rooms of the country.

I have tried to tell the opinions of many because I would mistrust the man who knew the truth for certain. A fellow Yorkshireman, Michael Parkinson, put Boycott's case as positively as any, writing in the *Sunday Times*. He believes the basic premise is that Boycott does not want

D

to play for England because he has no faith in those who run the national team, and no regard for Denness under whom he was asked to play.

'Like all perfectionists he is obsessive about his own standards, meticulous in his assessment of other players and to ask him to serve under someone who falls short of his requirements is like asking Field Marshal Montgomery to be a lance-corporal in Fred Karno's army. The important question raised by Geoffrey Boycott's refusal to play for England is not about the man, but about the way the game is run.

'The purblind mandarins at Lord's, joined at the hip by the majority of cricket commentators, will tut-tut about that bounder Boycott while ignoring the basic fundamental question he has posed. Boycott has challenged the hypocrisy of English cricket and will no doubt pay the price, but unless the lesson is learned the game will be the final loser.'

So there is the division and the sadness. Possibly the greatest sadness has reached Boycott himself, who realises that if he had continued as England's opener when fears of ill-health, because he has no spleen, persuaded him to cry off as my vice-captain in India and Pakistan in 1972–3, Mike Denness would not have been selected for that tour at all. Then again, if he had continued under Denness a short while longer he might have succeeded when Tony Greig did.

Who is to say that Geoff Boycott would have made a good England captain? Or will? Was Mike Denness as bad as the criticism heaped upon him suggested? Briefly, Denness led MCC to a drawn series in West Indies after Ray Illingworth had lost to them at home just months before. He defeated India who had beaten us in two successive series before that, and drew with Pakistan at home. Finally, he lost mainly to the shattering fast bowling of Lillee and Thomson in Australia before defeating New Zealand in a two-match series out there.

His 188 in the sixth Test against Australia without Thomson, and virtually without Lillee, proved that pace was the crucial difference between winning and losing; but apart from that it was the highest innings by an England captain in a Test in Australia, exceeding A. E. Stoddart's 173, also in Melbourne, in 1894–5. Criticism of Denness's captaincy has often masked his ability as a batsman.

Whatever Geoff Boycott's initial upset, it has now become an illness; nothing will persuade the patient that he has not taken a blow, or that the cause will be better served on the international field rather than off it. There is a leaden finality about the situation which no one appears to have the power to lift.

7 *Goodbye Cowdrey?*

TO RETIRE ...

June 9th

No cricketer in my experience has been applauded to the crease more often than Colin Cowdrey, who has announced that he is retiring at the end of the season. Whether he emerges from the pavilion at Tunbridge Wells or Taunton, or even, contrary to some who perpetuate North versus South prejudices, in Scarborough where I watched him bat last summer, there is an aura about his arrival which prompts great expectancy from the spectators.

Just imagine how many times since his first-class debut in 1950 he has emerged from the dressing room to a warm Kentish reception. How many soaking wet garlands have been flung around his neck in Pakistan; how often small packets of rice have burst at his feet as he walked to bat into a white-hot Indian stadium. Or in Australia where, hard-arsed unromantics that the natives claim to be, he was fêted with continuous applause even before he had completed that superlative first Test century against the Aussies at Melbourne in 1954–55.

The aura that surrounds him has nothing to do with physical presence as it has been with Ted Dexter or with Tony Greig. Cowdrey's heavy figure moves sedately to the crease, shoulders sloping and slightly hunched, padding like an amiable Womble.

He has never lost the schoolboy chubbiness, though a swarthy skin tells something of 118 Test matches and 105 first-class centuries. There is much more of the schoolboy in him than just looks. He may be retiring at the end of this season, but he would go on much longer if Kent wished it. Nothing would make him happier than to play for Kent with his son, and indeed his grandson; share their jokes, and drink cool beers in blazer and flannels on pavilion steps and talk about the great art, the only art—batsmanship.

I first went to his house on the Kent-Surrey border about ten years ago with some Glamorgan colleagues. We had generous hospitality and home movies of Harold Larwood bowling. Then, in the garden, in the family practice net we studied the automatic bowling machine.

'Get inside the game,' Cowdrey advised. 'Explore the theories, experiment with the lot and then, with careful thought, fine it all down to simplicity. That is the answer to batting . . . surely?'

There have been many times in his career when Cowdrey's batting has looked strangled by theory. The use of the pad against spin bowling often restricted his power. Yet he would always emerge eventually with the proper strength which comes from perfect timing.

At his best he could be cruelly destructive without jerking a single muscle, though sometimes he becomes so passive—just like going through a beautiful but fruitless exercise. Add to this young view of the game his enviable talent, his gentle character and projection as the English gentleman and it is easy to understand how his charm has won him admirers all over the world, as well as odd critics among the more hardened professionals.

It is wrong in his case to equate a ready smile and public school politeness with a soft centre. Without enormous ambition he would never have secured his fame. What triumph it was for him to be selected by the MCC players last winter to join them. They met and resolved that the best player of true fast bowling in England, even at the age of 42, was Colin Cowdrey. They must have him alongside them.

There is a saying in cricket circles that 'it's what you

do in the middle that counts'. Colin Cowdrey has done almost all that can be done and therefore earned acclaim of fellow-players.

Yet being Colin Cowdrey suits him, too. He is superb at the arduous duties.

In my mind's eye I see him addressing the school assembly at 7.15 in the morning in a Ceylon college; reading the lesson in church in Sydney; laughing and joking with a tight-lipped maharajah who is neither laughing nor joking; writing letters daily to all persons from all parts, congratulations, commiserations and encouragements.

I was fielding 15 yards away from him at Maidstone in May, 1969, when his Achilles tendon snapped. It was a sickening sound. He was 37 and it was generally thought to be the end of his career. Back he came. Why? The boyish enthusiasm had not waned. The record book had to be put right, too—the hundred hundreds were not complete.

'When you are beaten by a ball, you must kick yourself,' he once told me as we drove in his easily-recognised Jaguar with MCC number plate, through the lanes of Kent. 'You must say "Gosh! that ball almost got me. What did I do wrong? I must get that right." You must look forward to the next ball or else you should retire.'

I do not believe that he has retired for that reason. With Kent he probably cannot get enough cricket—a domestic sadness.

We drove on through Westerham and stopped and studied the huge sculpture of Sir Winston Churchill reclining. Then on to Chartwell to marvel at the walls the great man himself built when he had retreated from the House. Cowdrey and Churchill would have been near neighbours. Without Sir Winston's famed irascibility, I think Colin Cowdrey has always shared the same urge to draw large lines on the world which he himself has learned to master.

June 27th

From an apparently hopeless position—they needed 354 to win in five and a quarter hours—Kent cut down Australia with a memorable flourish at Canterbury and the man who warmed everyone with the sight of a great innings was Colin Cowdrey.

It was his 106th century and made on the day when it was announced that he will captain MCC against Australia at Lord's in a week's time. Why does he not retire quietly instead of plaguing the Test selectors with performances of virtuosity like this? Should he get runs in that match, is it such a stray thought to imagine his name on the table when the England captaincy is decided next week? This captaincy is meant to be a gesture of thanks before his retirement.

There was the heartening sight too of Australian fieldsmen running to shake the old maestro by the hand at the end of this rapturous 151 not out (I must try to limit my superlatives but it will be difficult).

The runs flowed over a fast outfield from a pitch offering a little spin but no spite. Lillee sent down bouncers but they were firmly hooked; balls outside the off-stump were impudently smoothed down fine of third man, or cut square of him; the leg spin was directed powerfully through the cover field and the off-spinner Ashley Mallett was tucked and turned away through so many corners on the leg side it scarcely mattered where the fielders were standing.

In all this Cowdrey was aided with plenty of courage and skill, if not matching grandeur, by Nicholls and Woolmer. Dennis Lillee was a remarkable combination of subtle and unsubtle tactics. There was a time when he seemed intent only on trying out his bouncers on a patient Luckhurst. Occasionally he tossed in a leg-spinner or even yet another bouncer, off a short run. He is a marvellous athlete and one of the very finest bowlers, but he, Woolmer, Alan Turner who got 156 in the tourists' first innings, and all on the field, had to acknowledge that their efforts were lost in the glare of an exceptional Cowdrey offering, which led Kent to victory by 4 wickets.

... OR NOT TO RETIRE?

Saturday, June 28th

Colin Cowdrey has been asked by Sussex to join them next season; at least Tony Greig has telephoned Cowdrey with the offer which we hear is being strongly considered.

His retirement from Kent one day and his renaissance with Sussex the next must confuse and perhaps rankle Kentish folk, who have always felt the player and the County to be inseparable. After his regal 151 not out on Friday against Australia, in their minds it must be as if Canterbury Cathedral was being uprooted and shifted to Brighton.

Of course nothing can debar a cricketer from earning his living with any county once a proven deadlock exists between him and his employers; as it was in Ray Illingworth's case, or if the employers no longer wish to offer him work. Ever since the Barry Knight case was fought by the legal men from Leicester and his departure from Essex was secured, the principle that no restraint of trade be allowed in cricket was established. Yet it broke down County loyalties which is sad for the romantic affiliations many followers build up. (However would the old cigarette card publishers cope?) To me it was unthinkable that someone as Yorkshire, in voice and thought, as Ray Illingworth should not play out his career in Bradford, Leeds, Middlesbrough and all points north of Pontefract.

For Colin Cowdrey it is a different matter. He first announced his retirement, then came the call from Tony Greig. The motivation was honourably made in the interests of Kent. He would have liked to have played more cricket for them, and was not offered it. His relationships with the club have soured since his days of captaincy. Yet he did not wish to stand in the way of young players either.

At the age of 42 he will ponder long and hard about the prospect of joining Sussex.

What can he hope for? Will his talent stand up? His initial thoughts were these before his hundred at Canterbury.

'Everyone says that Jack Hobbs and others have gone on until they are fifty . . . but look how they were built physically; nice and lean, not a lot of weight to carry. What is the point in going to accept a challenge if you may not be chipping in enough to help?'

What now? If I were Colin Cowdrey, I would recognise that performance *does* decline. Talented young players often score good-looking twenties; talented veterans do also. The graph rises and falls. In his case it is not just a simple case of continuing a career, it is of prolonging it and yet retaining its authority. It is almost a treacherous situation for him. How can a man of talent, who cannot refuse a cricketing challenge, possibly do anything but dream of scattering the seagulls at Hove and making nodding senior citizens in deckchairs sit up and take notice. On the form he struck at Canterbury this week, he will have them queueing at the gates.

July 4th, MCC *v* Australia

First innings: M. C. Cowdrey lbw bowled Lillee o.
Second innings: M. C. Cowdrey caught Gilmour bowled Lillee o.
Well, I suppose Don Bradman, himself bowled Hollies for a duck in his last match against England, would approve . . . if this was, in fact, Colin Cowdrey's last against Australia. But who can be sure of that!

8 Benson & Hedges Cup Final: Leicestershire v Middlesex

MIDDLESEX

M. J. Smith	c Tolchard, b Booth	83
P. H. Edmonds	c Illingworth, b McVicker	11
C. T. Radley	c Higgs, b McVicker	7
J. M. Brearley	c Davison, b McVicker	2
N. G. Featherstone	c Tolchard, b McVicker	11
H. A. Gomes	b Higgs	3
G. D. Barlow	b Illingworth	7
J. T. Murray	c Cross, b Steele	1
F. J. Titmus	run out	0
M. W. W. Selvey	c Tolchard, b Booth	6
J. S. E. Price	not out	2
Extras (lb 10, nb 3)		13
	Total	146

Overs: 52.4.
Fall of wickets: 1-26, 2-37, 3-43, 4-87, 5-99, 6-110, 7-117, 8-119, 9-141.
Bowling: McKenzie 7-2-20-0, Higgs 10-3-18-1, McVicker 11-3-20-4, Booth 8.4-1-25-2, Cross 2-0-9-0, Illingworth 9-1-3-1, Steele 5-0-10-1.

LEICESTERSHIRE

B. Dudlestone	run out	17
J. F. Steele	c Selvey, b Titmus	49
J. C. Balderstone	run out	12
B. F. Davison	c Murray, b Gomes	0
R. W. Tolchard	not out	47
G. F. Cross	lbw, b Titmus	0
R. Illingworth	not out	13
Extras (b 3, lb 9)		12
	Total (5 wkts)	150

Overs: 51.2.
Fall of wickets: 1-32, 2-67, 3-67, 4-118, 5-121.
Bowling: Price 9-3-26-0, Selvey 9.2-2-33-0, Titmus 11-2-30-2, Gomes 11-4-22-1, Edmonds 11-2-27-0.
Umpires: W. L. Budd, A. E. Fagg.
Leicester won by 5 wickets.

Accompanied by the usual Cup Final clatter, banners waving, bells ringing and an anthology of battle chants, of which 'Illy for England' and 'Nice wun Norman' topped the pops, Ray Illingworth accepted the Benson & Hedges Cup on Leicestershire's behalf after a prolonged but not truly nailbiting contest.

Leicestershire won by five wickets in the 52nd over. The total to be overtaken was 146, which may seem modest, but in fact was the fruit of steady graft by Mike Smith, who batted until the 51st over.

Judging by the struggle everyone had at the crease, the low bounce and the slow pace of the pitch prevented the batting dominance which most supporters of one-day cricket enjoy best.

Middlesex had reached the final in Houdini style and they can feel a sense of achievement at reaching this lofty stage. Not since 1949, when they shared the County Championship, have honours come their way. Leicestershire, on the other hand, claim that this particular Benson & Hedges Cup is theirs by divine right. They won it in the first year and were runners-up last time. However, it was the memory of that particular defeat which might have haunted them most. It was a low scoring final last year and they managed only 143 runs, batting second.

Middlesex won the toss and batted first under grey skies. After half an hour, drizzling rain arrived and play was stopped for 40 minutes. When they resumed it was difficult to tell whether the batsmen were suffering problems of 're-entry' or whether the wicket was indeed low and slow. The problems Mike Smith had, even allowing for the fact that he may have been a little below best form, made it obvious that often the ball struck too low on the bat to trouble the fielders.

It was in this early period, too, that Norman McVicker was bowling well enough to earn the Man of the Match award. He bounded in, in his easy style, just three men on the leg side, as he wheeled away just on or outside the off stump. He trapped four of the first five batsmen but not without the aid of excellent fielding. Illingworth caught Edmonds at cover. It was a misdrive, which curled and dipped slightly and the captain did well to pick it up against a lively background. 'Nice wun Norman. Let's have another wun' they chanted. Obliging lad that he is, he found the edge of Radley's bat—a key wicket this—had him cutting too close to the stumps and Higgs took the catch. Then Brearley, another man in form and a fine competitor, fell to one of the finest catches I have seen for many a season.

His firm drive rose just a foot above ground level, a certain four to cover's left. But there lurked another competitor, Davison, who dived in a flash, scooping up the ball as it was about to hit the ground. Many would have stayed to question it. Brearley was happy and departed.

Featherstone was next, caught behind and there were few moments when Middlesex looked in control. Leicestershire were every bit a winning side in the field. They opened up with just a couple of slip fielders to McKenzie and two slips to Higgs. It was an attritious approach, perfectly carried out by players who have been fired and hardened in this sort of competition.

In the interval a brief spin around the ground by the band of the Coldstream Guards prompted the comment that they were no better than the Coalville Colliery band, and that, not surprisingly, from a Midlands gent, who claimed to know his cornet spittle better than most. Whatever the musical quality, they set a handsome scene for Leicestershire's run chase.

Steele and Dudleston put on 32 runs by nudge, by flick and deflection. Two run-outs then changed Middlesex's rather gloomy prospects.

Dudleston charged off on a run he was not called for and Balderstone failed to beat Barlow's underarm throw which broke the stumps. Davison was caught behind without score, so at 67–3 Middlesex began to wonder if predestination was yet a living doctrine.

Roger Tolchard destroyed any illusions. His running between the wickets with Steele raised the whole tempo of the innings. Pressures were put on fielders—Radley dived and saved a few runs, Brearley dived and missed, while Titmus found the pace just a little too hot.

However, with the ball, both Titmus and Edmonds posed their problems but the tide was taking the game away from them. Middlesex will look back and regret that their key batsmen had not come off together.

Runs never came from both ends and that is not quite good enough to hold off the worthy specialists, and in this cricket no one is more special than Roger Tolchard.

'Back to the road, and I crossed again,
Over the miles of the saltbush plain—
The shining plain that is said to be
The dried-up bed of an inland sea.
Where the air so dry and so clear and bright
Refracts the sun with a wondrous light,
And out in the dim horizon makes
The deep blue gleam of phantom lakes.'
History books tell us how the huge expanse of Australia
has fashioned a hardy race, certainly in those outbacks
described in verse by 'Banjo' Paterson. Mind you, that I
read any 'Banjo' at all is due to Jack Fingleton who eyed
what he called a 'Welsh druid' in the Press box and
obviously thought 'The fella probably thinks we've no
poetry in our souls.' I am grateful to the maestro for this
small guidance.

Life in the cities, like Edwardian Sydney for example,
is obviously more genteel than up-country, but the
attitudes of Australian cricketers on the field suggests a
pride in living up to the legend of the raw life—tough
and extrovert like Keith Miller, taciturn like Bill Lawry,
or just a hard-arsed word slinger like Chappelli, as
Australia's 1975 captain is known. That most affectionate
scribe R. C. Robertson-Glasgow described W. J.
O'Reilly as having 'the face and form such as you might
have seen in a picture of explorers or pioneers', and
C. V. Grimmett was simply 'compounded of tea, leather,
patience and subtlety'.

The manner in which Dennis Lillee, Jeff Thomson and

Max Walker attacked MCC's batsmen last winter suggests they had been banished beforehand to a saltbush plain, lean, hungry, lolling under gaunt gum trees swatting the flies, and waiting for the call to Brisbane. It was there, on November 29th, 1974, that they began their long reign of terror. It is no exaggeration. Batsmen returned to England convinced that they had never experienced pace like it, nor bounce—and the two together are nearly always deadly. Worse even than that, as far as this new four-match series in England was concerned, their nerve was broken. At Brisbane, to be fair, the Lord Mayor prepared the pitch badly—'come into my parlour said the spider to the fly'. In went Dennis Amiss, the world's outstanding run-scorer at the time, and he retreated with a bone in his finger broken by Thomson. Edrich, second top-scorer in the English innings with 48, was hit by Lillee. He too had broken a bone in the hand and both players missed the second Test. The series had begun to the echo of superb gamesmanship by Dennis Lillee on television. 'I use the bouncer to hit the batsman somewhere between the rib-cage and the stomach,' he confessed.

It was a malicious opening to a rubber though England were the first to start the glut of short bowling. Willis and Lever were as much to blame, but were nothing like as fast as Lillee and Thomson. Nor was Max Walker to be underestimated either. Standing 6 ft. 3 in. and well built, he extracted almost as much awkward bounce as the others.

The demise of English batsmanship in Australia which followed is the subject of other books, yet it is important to realise what mental grip Australia had on England before this new series can be understood.

One must recall the curve of hawk-like fielders around every English bat, the goal-keeping acrobatics performed behind the stumps by Rod Marsh as the balls literally took-off from bone-hard ground, the almost un-precedented shower of mockery and bad language which passed mainly from Australia to England, as well as the English bats which flashed almost involuntarily outside the off-stump, offering snicks to be gobbled up by skilled, prehensile fingers.

England won one Test match when Jeff Thomson was absent injured, and Dennis Lillee bowled only six overs because of a foot injury. One was drawn, four were lost heavily, and the English captain, Mike Denness, was forced to drop himself. There are few drubbings more painful than that, and now, only months later, with the fun of the Prudential Cup behind them, England were going to be pushed into the ring again, by administrators who believed Australia's presence in this country for the one-day competition, was too good to waste.

For the English public it was an exciting prospect. Fast bowlers have always attracted crowds. The sight of a Larwood, Lindwall, Tyson or Lillee racing in and sending a ball whistling past the batsman's nose is a breathtaking, sanguine but splendid experience . . . for those watching.

However, there was the prospect that the millions waiting both in England and Australia to view the contest on television would be disappointed. Negotiations had been going on for many months between the BBC and the Test and County Cricket Board only to reach deadlock.

Even the closest of cricket followers were confused and split on the issue, which was all to do with the price required by the Board being far in excess of what the BBC were prepared to put up. £95,000 was offered by the BBC, and some saw it as folly that the TCCB should claw away for more at the risk of losing the BBC's support altogether. The BBC's contribution to cricket in 1975 is over £200,000, and the counties, eternally on the breadline, cannot afford to lose that. Were they not prodding the golden goose too hard by asking for £160,000 for the four Tests?

In 1972 the BBC paid £24,000 per Test for the Ashes series. This year, then, they were being asked for £40,000 a Test to keep pace with inflation. This was also an effort by the TCCB to put a realistic value on cricket. The next move was the BBC's who stated that their offer was to be £95,000 which is £23,750 a Test, less than in 1972! So the battle raged and the prospect of all the young cricketers of the country being able to savour the skills of the great fast bowlers was vanishing fast.

The BBC argued with some justification that they surely deserved to get the 'cream' of the season if they were sinking that £200,000 into the rest of the cricket. If they withdrew that, the sponsors, Benson and Hedges, Gillette and John Player would be bound to withdraw their support too. Also the BBC were bound by severe budget restrictions.

The outcome is well-known, but it made an interesting test case. The TCCB offered three Tests only at a cost of £90,000. The BBC came back with £115,000 for four, which was rejected. £120,000 for the four was finally settled which included the rights to televise morning play live to Australia. That figure also happened to be the maximum money available but it did lead the way to a deal of £150,000 being done for the West Indies series in 1976.

For the very first time the TCCB had made a brave effort to evaluate cricket. They had much to lose, but no doubt encouraged by the record attendances which were building up at Sunday League matches, and the colossal success of the Prudential competition, they felt it wrong in the interests of cricket to sell the game short. So the scene was set, all eyes were on Edgbaston. Mike Denness won the toss for England and told Ian Chappell he would like to have discussion with his senior players before deciding to bat or field.

AUSTRALIA

R. B. McCosker	b Arnold	59
A. Turner	c Denness, b Snow	37
*I. M. Chappell	c Fletcher, b Snow	52
G. S. Chappell	lbw, b Old	0
R. Edwards	c Gooch, b Old	56
K. D. Walters	c Old, b Greig	14
†R. W. Marsh	c Fletcher, b Arnold	61
M. H. N. Walker	c Knott, b Snow	7
J. R. Thomson	c Arnold, b Underwood	49
D. K. Lillee	c Knott, b Arnold	3
A. A. Mallett	not out	3
Extras (b 1, lb 8, nb 9)		18
		359

Fall of wickets: 1-80, 2-126, 3-135, 4-161, 5-186, 6-265, 7-286, 8-332, 9-343.
Bowling: Arnold 33-3-91-3, Snow 33-6-86-3, Old 33-7-111-2, Greig 15-2-43-1, Underwood 7-3-10-1.

ENGLAND

J. H. Edrich	lbw, b Lillee	34	c Marsh, b Walker		5
D. L. Amiss	c Thomson, b Lillee	4	c sub (Gilmour) b Thomson		5
K. W. R. Fletcher	c Mallett, b Walker	6	c Walters, b Lillee		51
*M. H. Denness	c G. S. Chappell, b Walker	3	b Thomson		8
G. A. Gooch	c Marsh, b Walker	0	c Marsh, b Thomson		0
A. W. Greig	c Marsh, b Walker	8	c Marsh, b Walker		7
†A. P. E. Knott	b Lillee	14	c McCosker, b Thomson		38
D. L. Underwood	b Lillee	10	b Mallett		3
C. M. Old	c G. S. Chappell b Walker	13	c Walters, b Lillee		7
J. A. Snow	lbw, b Lillee	0	c Marsh, b Thomson		34

G. G. Arnold	not out	0	not out	6
Extras (lb 3, w 5, nb 1)		9	(b 2, lb 5, nb 2)	9
		101		173

Fall of wickets: 1-9, 2-24, 3-46, 4-46, 5-54, 6-75, 7-78, 8-87, 9-97.

1-7, 2-18, 3-20, 4-52, 5-90, 6-100, 7-122, 8-151, 9-167.

Bowling: Lillee 15-8-15-5, Thomson 10-3-21-0, Walker 17.3-5-48-5, Mallett 3-1-8-0.

Second innings: Lillee 20-8-45-2, Walker 24-9-47-2, Thomson 18-8-38-5, Mallett 13.2-6-34-1.

Umpires: A. E. Fagg, H. D. Bird.

Toss won by England.

Australia won by an innings and 85 runs.

Australia's team selection was no problem. It was based on loyalty to players who have done the trick in the past, and also the knowledge that their very appearance on the field was likely to bring old skeletons out of the English cupboards. Gary Gilmour had bowled more impressively than Jeff Thomson on the tour, but he was the one omitted from the twelve.

England arrived at the ground with thirteen players, eleven of whom had been through the winter nightmare. The new men were Graham Gooch, 21, a bold selection based on his form for Essex and his innings of 75 for MCC against the tourists at Lord's. It must have brought a nod of satisfaction from those who cared for his cricket at Norlington Junior High School in Leyton, and indeed from those who, in the National Cricket Association, scheme tirelessly to raise funds to establish international competition at youth level. Gooch was a member of the England Young Cricketers side of 1972 which toured the West Indies.

The other newcomer was Bob Woolmer, 27, the Kent all-rounder. Most of his career since his debut in 1968 has been spent in the lower order of the Kent batting. He revealed nothing extra-special in three-day cricket but the combination of a good range of strokes with the bat, and nagging accuracy with the ball, had raised him above the ordinary as a one-day player. Indeed he had already played for England in Prudential matches. Two factors had much to do with his recognition as a Test player. First, Mike Denness had the good sense to raise Woolmer in the Kent batting order from the start of the season. Secondly, Woolmer himself had done much to improve the straightness of his batting by going out to South Africa to coach and play. He represented Natal during the 1973–74 season.

However, as it turned out, Denness chose to leave out Woolmer as well as Hendrick. He announced his team to Ian Chappell as Amiss, Edrich, Fletcher, Gooch, Denness, Greig, Knott, Old, Snow, Underwood, Arnold. The Australian captain responded with—McCosker, Turner, I. Chappell, G. Chappell, Edwards, Walters, Marsh, Walker, Thomson, Lillee, Mallett.

It was at this point that Denness sought advice with the toss which he had won. Clouds chased each other around the Edgbaston ground, one of the rare days all summer that the sun was not shining down.

I would not pretend to know who advised what, but the news soon came over the loudspeakers that Australia had been put in to bat. The arguments which supported this were clear, but not overwhelming. In such conditions the ball might move about in the air, and also find deviation off the pitch which could be holding early moisture. Not only could England expect to get wickets, they would also be denying Lillee, Thomson and Walker the conditions in which they would thrive. The pain of previous batting disasters was not a very welcome prospect on a chill, dull day, right at the start of a new series. The job of batting last on a wicket known to get slower and more benign as the match progressed was quite inviting too. Mallett was the only spinner to trouble them if the surface wore badly.

Thus the die was cast, but one old adage of the cricket

world was by-passed. 'Never "insert" the opposition if there is rain about.'

On that first day Australia made 243 for 5 before rain concluded play 17 minutes before 6.30 p.m. Honours were fairly even though the initial gambit had not wholly come off. Rick McCosker and Alan Turner batted safely through the morning putting on 77 runs. The England bowlers pitched a little short of a length and found a powder-puff bounce. The ball seamed, but slowly. McCosker, watchful at first, proceeded to play handsome strokes outside the off-stump where he is reputedly edgy. Old looked the likeliest to take a wicket but it was Snow after lunch who persuaded Turner to pull a ball of unsuitable length into the hands of Denness at mid-wicket.

English hearts leapt higher half-way through the afternoon when Old got the true dessert for his full length bowling by trapping Greg Chappell lbw for nought. Then later in the day, after Ian Chappell had played an innings of skill before falling to a fine catch at first slip, the score of 186 for 5 left the issue open. However, these were England's last moments of hope and indeed the last days of Test captaincy for Mike Denness.

Rod Marsh, Ross Edwards and Jeff Thomson all applied themselves successfully to the job of extending their sides score to 359. It was an innings which underlined how well their talents mix. When a show of aggression was required Ian Chappell was there to provide it; when good sense was essential Edwards and Marsh knew exactly how to defend firmly without losing the obvious opportunities to thump fours. Jeff Thomson added that touch of bravado which Lillee so often does, and swung merrily to the discomfort of England's faster bowlers.

Indeed Thomson's adventures suggested that movement had left the wicket altogether, and although one realised that the English batsmen could not exactly be looking forward to renewing acquaintances with their winter 'undertakers', there was reasonable hope if the first hour could be seen off.

As Amiss and Edrich walked to the middle—Amiss, eyes to the ground in the knowledge that there was now no escape, and Edrich, jauntily as ever, though probably feeling the same—the sky was darkening and filling in. After one over from Dennis Lillee, thunder arrived and brought a storm which flooded the square. The wicket, of course, is covered only at the ends. England's watery grave was prepared.

At first, it was impossible to tell how the ball was likely to respond to the sticky surface, mainly because Jeff Thomson sent four of his first ten balls for wides. He was replaced by Walker after two overs and the signs were then clear. Walker swung the ball and got increasing lift from the pitch as it dried. Lillee got the ball up twice as high as anyone had managed in the Australian innings. An hour and 40 minutes had been lost, which meant that an extra hour was to be added on to the end of the day, taking play through to 7.30 p.m. Now, almost certainly, there was no escape.

For nine overs the openers held them off, then Amiss popped a ball off his glove into the hands of Thomson at backward short-leg. Fletcher fenced a lifting ball into the hands of gully, but Denness inspired more confidence as Edrich 'did his own thing', as he always does, at the other end. Denness nearly always starts an innings well because he moves his feet much more smartly than others backwards or forwards. He has had unfair criticism for the initial move he takes backwards with the rear foot before coming into line. Technically it does not reveal a chicken-heart. On the contrary, I have seen Denness play extremely brave innings on nasty wet wickets for Kent. He threatened to do so here for England, until Walker got one to move away off the pitch, and he was gone at second slip after a fifty minute fight.

In a way it was a good moment for young Gooch to make his Test debut. If he collected thirty or forty runs on this strip he would be a success, yet no one could blame him for failing. He moved solidly across behind the line, almost too far and too soon, it appeared to some. Two balls later those cognoscenti were saying 'I told you so'. Gooch tickled one of Walker's least dangerous deliveries into Marsh's waiting gloves down the leg side. Would Greig's height give him any advantage? For a moment it looked as if it would, and he was cheeky enough to lift Walker almost for six over mid-on. The next ball he glanced for four. This was the Greig who had lifted our hearts during those early morning broadcasts from Australia. Next ball . . . an injudicious guiding shot, hopefully aimed to third man, but destined for Marsh's safe grasp. 54 for 5. Edrich played and missed but rode his luck and Alan Knott came in to hop about all over the crease, dropping the lifting ball into the blockhole with a great show of determination but no back-lift.

The return of Lillee to the attack ripped deeper into the carcass. He was faster than any others, possibly the run-ups were firmer than they had been after the rain. Whatever the conditions, he needed no other spur than the sight of an English sweater twenty-two yards away. He attacks with his mind, his body, his superlative action and his harsh, cutting vocabulary. Like all the finest quick bowlers his action gathers momentum. His feet tear away at the ground and his lean body rushes faster to its energetic conclusion. His black hair blows behind him, but his head is steady; it must be to be as accurate as he is. A batsman really has to sense where his off stump is unless he cares to make a pass at those balls whistling past just outside. It was in this spell that he bowled Knott with a ball that looked too good by half, and brought one back off the wicket to catch Edrich lbw without playing a stroke. 83 for 7, on a wicket which now gave the batsmen no chance at all, and three days to go.

A large crowd gathered on the Saturday to witness what they dreamed might be a glorious fight-back, a lash in the tail to save the follow on, 77 runs away, and perhaps a faint roar from the lions on the chest to suggest that we were not to be pushed around in our own country. Yet the action continued like a bad thriller. Every horror was totally predictable, no sleight of hand, no trickery, just plain murder by the Australians, with English corpses heaped up in their wake. In 24 minutes England were all out and informed that they would have to bat again, 258 required to avoid the innings defeat. There was an early morning sun, but a layer of high cloud when play began. Alan Smith, Warwickshire's former captain, predicted on Friday that the wicket would seam about as it dried, while Ted Dexter, with whom I played golf on the nearby Edgbaston course early that morning, felt that it was humid enough to swing. I agreed with him. It was hot and rather oppressive.

Well, we all know how wrong we can be about those matters. It was a question of waiting for the evidence, and it was soon clear that movement off the seam was the threat.

Yet, I suppose, as Edrich and Amiss came out again hope sprang eternal. It was in the fifth over that Dennis Amiss showed for the first time, at least in this country, that his confidence against Lillee had gone. He turned his back on a ball which climbed from short of a length to about chest high and was struck such a painful blow on the elbow he had to retire. The call came for a doctor; the gremlins had once again struck down one of the batsmen who, if he got away to a solid start, could dictate to the opposition.

Edrich was soon with him in the dressing room. His luck had run out this time; no more playing and missing. This time the edge went safely to Marsh.

In came Mike Denness in place of young Gooch and I am sure I was not the only one who felt for him. It is hard enough to battle against that sort of attack on a wicket helping bowlers without having to be concerned that this might be your last chance for the moment to succeed as a captain/batsman. Mike Denness has battled against many odds, off and on the field, as well as against the deficiencies of his batting which have only shown up against the fastest bowling. No one could have remained so outwardly philosophical about it all. Behind him, too, was a decision to field first in this match, which turned sour, ending in a débâcle for his side.

As ever he started well, firmly behind the ball and unafraid to play his shots. Then Thomson brought one back off the seam through his forward defence and it was all over with him. He looked to the skies and saw only pagan gods. 18 for 2 and enter Gooch with a 'duck' behind him. Within a minute he had become the third England player to 'bag a pair' on his Test debut, G. F. Grace (v Australia, The Oval 1880) and C. I. J. Smith (v West Indies, Bridgetown, 1934–35). It looked a fine delivery from Jeff Thomson which lifted and left the bat. Marsh rose superbly to take the catch high and wide.

After lunch the agonies heaped up. Greig carried the last realistic hopes of recovery. Walker promptly brought a ball back off the seam which touched the inside edge of Greig's bat. Marsh read the situation by instinct. Greig was gone.

Rain then fell heavily from 2.30 onwards. Everyone scattered for shelter or a beer, realising by this time that the resolute Fletcher, with Knott, had no chance of changing the course of Australia's fortunes. I went into the Ladbroke betting tent, squeezed past the punters and confirmed the lousy rumour. Yes, there it was, chalked up for all to see . . . England captain next Test, 1/3 Greig; 5/2 Denness; 6/1 Gilliat; 10/1 Edrich; and

20/1 Cowdrey. What a sordid state of affairs. The lynching parties had gathered before poor Denness had a chance to finish the game. The mood at Edgbaston is that he must go after 20 Tests as captain. Personally I shall applaud him from the international scene. It takes great strength in the soul to stare the hangman in the eye so often and dodge the rope completely, most recently by taking two big hundreds off New Zealand. Perhaps that is what his critics forgave him least of all!

When the teams returned at 4.35 the Australian attack continued its impressive destruction. They gave the batsmen few comfortable moments. Walker has the height and the action, unorthodox though it is, to hit the pitch hard just short of a length. The ball always appeared to be jarring the bat in the hands. Fletcher tucked one or two away off his legs, but there was little opportunity to play strokes with a full swing of the bat. Walker got plenty of movement off the seam too.

Jeff Thomson ran in as quickly as at any time on the tour. He does lose his line, but there were runs to play with and an umbrella of fielders to hang on to the snicks. There was no respite when he was bowling.

Yet I come back to Lillee. He was recalled to action at 5 o'clock as if he was in blind rage. I believe his relationship with Fletcher is less cordial than with most others, and by this time Fletcher had grafted his runs with the occasional scything cut deliberately directed over slip, and one flamboyant square cut off Lillee.

Lillee was not amused. He tore in even faster, stationed Edwards at fly-slip and then sent down a screaming short ball from which Fletcher twisted sharply away. It was a superb feat of evasion to a perfect fast bowling delivery. Yet Lillee was not to be denied his man. Another shortish ball, lifting rapidly just outside the off-stump, had Fletcher playing and running it to Walters who held the catch off his chest at third slip. What did Lillee screech at Fletcher as he departed? 'How's the wife and kids? See you in the bar Keith?' I think not, and England were left quietly turning on the spit at 93 for 5 over the weekend.

By lunch on the Monday the sun and wind were drying out the pitch at last, but there were only the last rites to perform. Knott again delayed the inevitable by his innings of 38 and Snow swung Mallett for a few sizeable blows to leg. At three o'clock in the afternoon Ian Chappell was generous in victory by saying that Australia would have been in similar trouble had they been forced to bat on such a wet wicket. He further voiced the opinion that Test match wickets should be covered in their entirety during playing hours.

A day later the England Selectors had changed their captain. Tony Greig was nominated for the three remaining Tests.

So Mike Denness steps down. Confining criticism purely to cricket in this first Test: there is no argument which has ever stood the test for putting in the opposition when there is rain about. Denness or May, Hutton or whoever—they would live to regret the decision which swung this game so horribly Australia's way.

Add, too, the reluctance to bowl the spinner. Only seven overs came from Underwood. Even if the ball was seaming on the first day, it was never doing it quickly enough to unsettle the likes of McCosker, Ian Chappell, Marsh or Thomson. Underwood is a bowler of flat trajectory but it was a variation worth trying.

However I must conclude by quoting Michael Melford of the *Daily Telegraph*, lest I get carried away with my own opinions. 'Meanwhile best wishes to all those, including myself, who in pub and power station, sauna bath and supermarket, must go on captaining England impeccably from a distance and with hindsight. It is a difficult job but, thank heavens, our prescience, tactical genius, powers of leadership and spirit of aggression are up to it.'

11   *Lord's—The Second Test*

ENGLAND

B. Wood	lbw, b Lillee	6	c Marsh, b Thomson	52
J. H. Edrich	lbw, b Lillee	9	c Thomson, b Mallett	175
D. S. Steele	b Thomson	50	c & b Walters	45
D. L. Amiss	lbw, b Lillee	0	c G. Chappell, b Lillee	10
G. A. Gooch	c Marsh, b Lillee	6	b Mallett	31
*A. W. Greig	c I. Chappell, b Walker	96	c Walters, b I. Chappell	41
†A. P. E. Knott	lbw, b Thomson	69	not out	22
R. A. Woolmer	c Turner, b Mallett	33	b Mallett	31
J. A. Snow	c Walker, b Mallett	11		
D. L. Underwood	not out	0		
P. Lever	lbw, b Walker	4		
Extras (b 3, lb 1, w 4, nb 23)		31	(lb 18, w 2, nb 9)	29
		315	7 wkts dec	436

Fall of wickets: 1-10, 2-29, 3-31, 4-49, 5-145, 6-222, 7-288, 8-309, 9-310.

1-111, 2-215, 3-249, 4-315, 5-380, 6-387, 7-436.

Bowling: Lillee 20-4-84-4, Thomson 24-7-92-2, Walker 21.4-7-52-2, Mallett 22-4-56-2.
Second innings: Lillee 33-10-80-1, Walker 37-8-95-0, Thomson 29-8-73-1, Mallett 36.4-10-127-3, I. M. Chappell 10-2-26-1, Walters 2-0-6-1.

AUSTRALIA

R. B. McCosker	c & b Lever	29	lbw, b Steele	79
A. Turner	lbw, b Snow	9	c Gooch, b Greig	21
*I. M. Chappell	c Knott, b Snow	2	lbw, b Greig	86
G. S. Chappell	lbw, b Snow	4	not out	73
R. Edwards	lbw, b Woolmer	99	not out	52
K. D. Walters	c Greig, b Lever	2		
†R. W. Marsh	c Amiss, b Greig	3		
M. H. N. Walker	b Snow	5		
J. R. Thomson	b Underwood	17		
D. K. Lillee	not out	73		

124

A. A. Mallett   lbw, b Steele   14
    Extras (lb 5, nb 6)   11   (lb 4, nb 14)   18

                        268   3 wkts   329

Fall of wickets: 1-21, 2-29, 3-37, 4-54, 5-56,   1-50, 2-169, 3-222.
6-64, 7-81, 8-133, 9-199.
Bowling: Snow 21-4-66-4, Lever 15-0-83-2, Woolmer 13-5-31-1, Greig 15-5-47-1, Underwood 13-5-29-1, Steele 0.4-0-1-1.
Second innings: Snow 19-3-82-0, Lever 20-5-55-0, Greig 26-6-82-2, Underwood 31-14-64-0, Woolmer 3-1-3-0, Steele 9-4-19-1, Wood 6-0-6-0.
Umpires: W. E. Alley, T. W. Spencer.
Toss won by England.
Match drawn.

England is at war with Australia. Is there anyone who doubts it? We have tasted physical intimidation and verbal intimidation and after the innings defeat at Edgbaston we are struggling to rescue national pride.

All sides bow to truly fast bowling and I would not suggest that this talented and rugged Australian side has too many weaknesses to probe unless it can be put under pressure. Yet it is now important for the English team and for all their supporters who live and die with them ball by ball, that they fight, talk about fighting and are seen to be fighting.

This is why the open aggression of Tony Greig, the new captain, suits the ignominious situation better than the gentle stoicism of Mike Denness. In truth we need a War Minister who alerts the country to the nature of the challenge and chooses colleagues whose optimism matches his own.

There was the feeling at Birmingham that the English batsmen were like veteran troops patched up after the winter campaign, but now asked once more to go 'over the top' to face the old nightmare.

Tony Greig has self-confidence. Back in India in 1972, even then he sensed the physical challenge of the next Australian series. 'It's going to be some series that, man,' he would say and duck an imaginary bouncer with a laugh.

When you think of it, he had to be sure he would not

lose his Test place in the meantime against New Zealand, West Indies at home, then West Indies away, as well as India and Pakistan at home, to speak out like that. Call it conceit if you like. It is what all cricketers need something of, and at this particular stage of the battle with Ian Chappell's side, the more of it the better.

Tony Greig has ability too, which is easily recognised and will silence the backbiting which stripped Mike Denness of one or two layers of authority. Though Denness, I should quickly add, averaged 42 in his eighteen matches as captain.

Greig can chip in to the action in so many ways—a slip catch, a fifty with the bat, an offspinner, an away-swinger. Yet there will be criticism. He has much to prove tactically and he may turn to his old mate Keith Fletcher, who reads the game so well; that is if Fletcher's self-confidence lasts the series. Personally I believe that Greig's captaincy will bring the best out of Fletcher, and Fletcher's presence will ensure that the new leader does not miss too many tactical tricks.

Much has been written about Greig's hot-headedness. I am not sure that he is impelled by anger as by refusal to be hemmed in by laws and etiquette. We laughed together the other day about his performance in that oven of a stadium, Madras.

He caught out Wadekar at second slip very clearly a couple of feet off the ground. Wadekar stood. The umpire at the bowler's end shook his head (which can mean many things in India) and walked to the square leg umpire.

For a moment there was an absurd threat that the decision may go against us. Greig raced across the square towards the adjudicators with the ball held high like a grenade with the pin out. The umpires were positively shaken by the sight. They conferred, Wadekar was out. It was an unruly performance but not without an amusing absurdity.

Other incidents like the running out of Kallicharan in the West Indies have created this aura of frenzy about Greig. Yet he is quick to acknowledge his own errors and is most certainly the man to have on your side.

His physical presence alone suggests authority and he has made himself the darling of the crowds by acting and reacting. This is the sort of man England needs in the crisis; someone who projects his will to win and his enthusiasm in the doing.

It is very much a Churchillian role: the elevation of a strong-minded individualist who, in times of prosperity on the field, would not be everyone's choice. Of Mike Denness he said, 'Mike did his very best. I lived with him abroad and I should know. You can't ask more of a man than he should give of his best.'

Does that not recall Churchill's vale to the peace-maker, Chamberlain, that he was 'prepared to strive continually in the teeth of the facts, face great risks for himself and his country'.

Players who talk of war are not always warlike. Tony Greig can back his words with actions, given the bounce of the ball which everyone needs. I just hope he can communicate it to all around him.

If he does, in fact, possess a touch of the Sir Winstons, he may greet Ian Chappell on the middle of Lord's with the famous words of 1941 'We will have no truce or parley with you, or the grisly gang who work your wicked will. You do your worst and we will do our best. Perhaps it may be our turn soon; perhaps it may be our turn now.' What he will probably say is 'Hello mate. We're going to stuff you this time.'

In old or new language, English followers will be refreshed to know that our chosen representatives are perhaps relishing the challenge, not dreading it.

To begin with, Greig walked towards the pavilion after the toss with Ian Chappell, then turned round to the groundsman's corner and indicated that he would like the use of the heavy roller. Relief rippled all round the packed ground. There were to be no more mysterious happenings attached to the drop of a coin in this match. The wicket was shorn of grass, a brown colour, and the sun shone.

I watched the morning's play from behind the bowler's arm high up in the pavilion stand. The ball did not swing, or bounce disconcertingly, yet Dennis Lillee had taken 4 wickets for 33 in his first 10 overs. Barry Wood had replaced Amiss as an opener, but he was lbw playing half forward to a ball which nipped back at him off the pitch. John Edrich too was lbw to the same bowler and Dennis Amiss, looking an uncertain shadow of the fine player he was a year ago, stumbled about the crease until he was trapped in front, lurking on the back foot to a ball well up to him. Umpire Alley was certainly in on the act—three lbws out of three. Amiss had not scored and Gooch played one shot of promise before edging a ball of good line to the keeper. Denness and Fletcher had been omitted and in at number three came a man who was to make a considerable impact on the series, David Steele.

In his long career with Northamptonshire he had grafted useful runs for many seasons, but without a hint of the class which one looks for in the best players. He proved on this very first morning in his very first Test that batting is about personality and character too. His habit of playing forward to all but the very short ball paid off, though he was quick to half-hook Lillee a couple of times down for boundaries to fine leg. The slowness of the pitch was the key to the whole game. It suited David Steele, and assisted also by Ian Chappell's persistence with attacking fields, he made quicker profit from his strokes than he might have in a normal day's county cricket. The lesson here is that unless you attack in the five-day game you will never bown out good

Lillee to Greig. 1st ball—a lucky inside edge for four

2nd ball—friendly discussion?

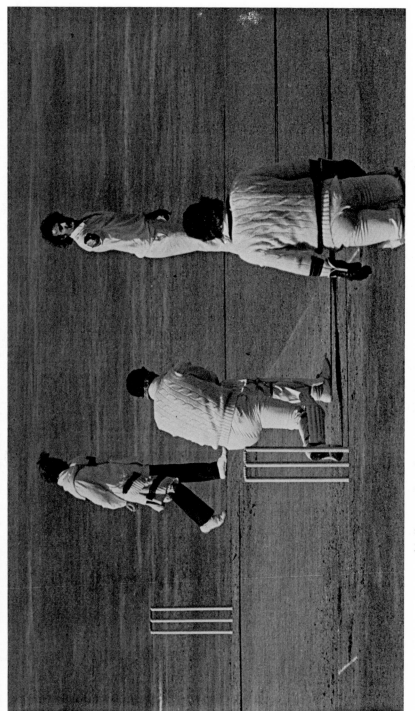

3rd ball—a cracking drive up to the advertisements at mid-off and the conversation hots up

Match abandoned. The day that the name of George Davis went into Wisden

'Welcome back' says Lillee. Graham Roope returned to the England side at the Oval after a 2 year absence

batsmen. Ian Chappell has brazen attacking instincts which have brought him ample return.

David Steele made 50 before he pulled a short ball from Thomson down on to his stumps. He had put on 96 with his captain Tony Greig who was playing the story-book captain's innings.

As Steele tucked and turned the ball away off the front foot, Greig leaned into handsome straight drives. Their instincts were different, understandably in the light of their comparative Test experience, but even if Steele had played a hundred Tests, the comparison would have been the same. It was interesting to see Lillee, Walker and Thomson cut down their speed, and Mallett come into the picture. Knott again chipped in a most valuable half century and down the order Woolmer had been included. The absentees were Old, who was twelfth man, and Arnold.

Thomson was no-balled 22 times in the first day and Ian Chappell was forced to debate the subject with umpire Alley. All in all, for England it had been a miracle day to keep Australia in the field from start to finish. The next morning matters were only prolonged a few minutes to make 315 the total.

Soon after lunch Australia were 81 for 7!

John Snow had taken four wickets, Peter Lever two, and Tony Greig one. Snow's performance was fascinating. His name will never be forgotten by Australians after his tour with Ray Illingworth in 1971–2. He was just about at his prime then, when he had genuine speed at his command. Nowadays his pace has been cut back and he has to persevere much more to get his wickets. In county cricket his attitudes have disappointed many who believe he does not try all the time. Possibly he is bored by doing the same thing every day of the week. Others have felt the same before him; it is just that more obvious in a fast bowler who is expected to rush in to bowl all the time.

Yet if he came into this Test series with doubts hanging over his menace with the new ball at the age of 33, it was soon obvious, as at Edgbaston, that the Australians had a serious respect for him. He was not going to be expensive, and furthermore he had not lost anything in the action. In fact, in 1973 when he last played for England, I thought his arm was low and slingy. It looked higher and more controlled now. He hit the seam on this lifeless Lord's wicket and most important of all kept the ball up to the bat. He varied his line from the bowling crease too. Alan Turner was the first to go, to a ball which Snow bowled from the Nursery end moving down the hill into the pads from outside the off-stump. In his sixth over Ian Chappell got another good one which had him caught at the wicket. In the seventh Greg Chappell, on the front foot, but not, it seemed very far forward, was lbw to one which came back.

After 65 minutes of clever controlled bowling on this sedate wicket Snow was replaced at the Nursery end by Lever. In his second over the man who had made it all look easy, Rick McCosker, played a false shot. He had been cutting strongly and thumping the ball firmly as ever through the on-side. Lever held one back, McCosker went for the drive and was caught and bowled. In Lever's next over Walters aimed a ferocious off-drive but edged the ball to Greig at first slip—a fast-moving, stinging catch.

The attitude of the English players was at first one of disbelief then, as each wicket fell, of triumph. Greig ran 'à la Benaud' to smack the lucky bowler on the back when wickets fell. He appeared to be employing the full repertoire of gamesmanship—waiting for Ian Chappell to settle at the crease before running the whole length of the pitch to chat to the bowler Snow. In every way he tried to heap on the agony and his last move before lunch was a classic in hustling. Greig himself came on at the pavilion end to bowl two overs before the interval. In his second, he ringed the determined, defensive Marsh with all sorts of short fielders. Marsh played forward, the ball hopped up off his pad, Amiss caught it at point. Everyone went up and he was given out, caught off bat and pad. Marsh did not agree with that decision. I should think the dressing room had cleared by the time he reached it, because he has earned quite a reputation as a bat-thrower in times of personal anger and disappointment.

Those decisions are terribly difficult to adjudicate with certainty. Bad ones turn a match sour in a second, and for every one that goes your way as the result of an appeal you know to be unjustified, it will be repaid you in similar fashion by your opponents sooner or later. Yet Marsh was gone, scattering members in the Long Room as he retreated.

Lord's was alive with chatter, optimistic, heady verbosity, presaging a miracle perhaps. My colleague from the *Daily Telegraph*, Michael Melford, who had been a witness of Australian domination for month after month, away and at home, gave a sigh and a smile and said it felt as if spring had come to Siberia.

Yet there is an Australian whom the Good Lord somehow fashioned for occasions like these, Ross Edwards by name. This 33-year-old, peace-loving, pipe-smoking gentleman, can be seen transformed on the field into a kamakazi fielder who hurls himself into the pickets so that he can scoop a ball back to keep it infield. He bats in similar mood—a crisis man. He shuffles across the stumps and tucks the ball around backward of square-leg. Any minute you expect a howl to go up for lbw. On this occasion, without risk or panic, he restored the proper balance between bat and ball on a slow uneventful wicket. Walker did not last long, but Edwards found allies in Lillee and Thomson. Thomson stayed for 65 minutes but it was Edwards who opened out. Snow tended later on to drop short and Edwards powered the ball to the square boundary on the off side. He approached his century with calm, it was inevitable, and he had no fears for Lillee who was batting with some relish. Then, however, he aimed a stroke through the on-side off a ball from Woolmer which was well up to the bat, and he was lbw—99 at Lord's, in what turned out to be his last appearance there! He will dream in years to come of that moment of error, and curse. It will never be put right, but then if all things could be righted, success would not be half as sweet in the batting game. It was an innings of the maximum importance not only in this match, but possibly in the series.

Lillee continued as if it was his personal 'benefit' match. He hooked Lever with a crunch for six in an over which cost twenty runs. Mallett blocked away at the other end, and when Australia were out—Mallett lbw to Steele—the collapse was repaired and only 47 runs separated the sides.

On Saturday England scored 230 for 2 and were 277 ahead, so the pace of their scoring from this point was crucial. John Edrich dominated the proceedings, scoring his seventh century against Australia—surpassed only by Hobbs, Hammond and Sutcliffe. It is also his twelfth hundred in his Test career and the 93rd in first-class cricket. It meant much to the confidence of Edrich himself. He played and missed many times but stuck doggedly to his mission—to wear down the fast bowlers who have terrorised England for many months. On Monday he carried his score to 175, the tempo increasing all the time as Greig looked for the declaration.

Ian Chappell had given the new ball to Max Walker, a departure from his normal habit, yet Wood, 52, survived confidently to put on 111 for the first wicket. Chappell never lost faith in his attacking field placings. Thomson looked faster than others. He got more bounce too with a slight breeze at his back on a lovely sunny day. Four slips, a gully, two backward short legs and forward—but no wickets came. David Steele followed Wood to the crease and he plunged on that front foot forward, a technique wholly suited to the wicket. Yet upon analysis his front foot play is crisp and he goes right forward. More important he again revealed a fighting Staffordshire heart. As England's number three in times of strife he is clearly the right man for the job.

It was almost incredible after a long stay that Steele should fall to Walters who took the second new ball. It was a full-toss, almost a loosener, and Steele miscued it straight back to the bowler.

Cricket's cruelties never surprise me. Indeed it was almost predictable that Dennis Amiss, hopefully sheltered from the full blast of pace at number four, should have to defend a 'pair' against Lillee with the new ball in his hand. He lasted out Saturday but was soon out, cutting at Lillee, Greg Chappell holding the catch at third slip.

Thereafter England's batsmen accelerated in fine style. Young Gooch picked up 31, which will have helped his confidence, because since his selection for England he has been unable to get any runs at all for Essex. Greig declared 483 runs ahead, leaving himself 500 minutes to bowl Australia out.

On the fifth and final day England needed the sort of luck the tourists had enjoyed with the weather at Edgbaston. Just before the match, when the wicket was fully covered, a thunderstorm fell at Lord's. If it had come an hour later after play had started, then only the ends would have been protected. As it was the start of play was delayed by an hour and a drawn match became inevitable barring another collapse by Chappell's men. When stumps were drawn the score was 329 for 3. England used seven bowlers; they clustered around the bat but met firm resistance, batting of real character from McCosker, the Chappell brothers and, of course, Ross Edwards.

England were rightly heartened, though they realised that on wickets where Lillee, Thomson and Walker are tamed, they themselves cannot hope to bowl out the opposition twice. Yet it is a turning point in optimism. Greig did marvellously well to put Australia under pressure at all, but once asked the question, the old green caps dropped over the pitch of the ball and batted out the message, that their side is not just made up of two fast bowlers. It is a team worthy of the country which cannot be hustled to defeat on a slow-flat wicket.

Lord's itself looked a picture. The gates were closed on more than one morning and apart from the rain which cost the game an hour's play on the last day, the sunshine was relentless, and just in case anyone was becoming slightly bored on Monday, a young man was generous enough to take off all his clothes and streak across the sacred square.

He hopped over the stumps with style. Umpire Tom Spencer beamed without moving, the police met him at the other side, held his arms, not roughly as if they were hauling him off to custody, but rather as if they had found an old mate and were insisting that he joined them for a pint in a little pub they knew down the road. All friendly stuff; nice looking lad too!

An Australian Test match at Lord's is the temple to which old cricketers repair, touch their caps to Old Father Time, 'Great Scorer', feast on the battles of the current generations, and slip out gems of comparison between their day and this. Old friends and foes lurk around every corner, reminiscing over lingering lunches in the marquée in the Rose Garden, which is properly coloured in MCC Yellow and Orange.

Middlesex's former captain, J. J. Warr, roams around with the confidence that he has a foot in both camps. He was one of the 'Magnificent Three'—Alec Bedser and Freddie Brown the others—who bowled through an Australian innings on the MCC tour of 1950–51 because both Trevor Bailey and Doug Wright were injured during the match. Now he is Australia's representative on the International Cricket Conference.

His humour is well known to all who have followed the sporting pages of the *Sunday Telegraph*. Seated next to the Chairman of Barclays Bank in one of the more decorous Tavern Stand boxes he was heard to remark: 'Well sir, I hope England's fine performance affects the level of the pound, because your sitting here at a time like this is rather like Sir Francis Drake playing bowls before the Armada!'

Sight of Freddie Brown, too, recalled the reputation he had in Australia as a leader of immense courage and of attacking instinct. Did they not sell lettuces on the streets in Sydney shouting: 'Lovely lettuces, fine lettuces, hearts as big as Freddie Brown.'

I am one of two from my old school, Neath Grammar, who played for England. The other man was there. Cyril Walters, whom many remember as the lean, languid caresser of fast bowling. He opened for England in five Tests against Australia in 1934, skippered the odd Test too.

With a twinkle in his eye he recorded his admiration for the modern player, their durability and physical strength to keep going day after day, winter and summer.

'I always got tired because I was not a strong man in my playing days,' he confessed. 'Would have loved to have kept going longer.'

The men with the agitated look are the selectors though they can be proud in their newest choices; Sir Len Hutton's mind may be a muddle of action replays of Lindwall and Miller, but he sees clearly the wisdom of playing fast bowling on the front foot as David Steele did.

This is a slow wicket, but many wickets fell to balls of fullish length which moved to beat players on the back-foot—Wood, Edrich, Amiss, Ian Chappell, for example.

'I was always afraid of the ball that came back off the

seam,' Sir Len admits. 'I found out that I could do nothing about that one if I went back. I don't understand this idea of going back and across, sometimes even before the ball is bowled.

'They might just as well stand plumb on the middle stump to start with.'

Out of all the jubilation, the nostalgia and the memories of great acts done before, came the strongest theme of constructive thought, that this Test match has everything but the art of flight.

With affection, the former England captain, R. E. S. Wyatt, described the leg-spin skills of Mailey, Grimmett, and South Africa's Balaskas.

'The quick arm action, the loop, spin imparted strong enough to drift the ball into the legs, and the bite to turn it across to the off when it pitched.' There ought to be hundreds of schoolboys practising the art of flight and spin in nets all over the country at the moment, because England's game lacks that important dimension.

And so conversations fondly drift to favourite subjects and the legends live in the presence of Gubby Allen, Denis Compton, Bill Edrich, Ted Dexter, Jim Laker, Ken Barrington, Richie Benaud, Trevor Bailey, Jack Fingleton and many more.

Yet even the greatest would agree that if only they knew then what they know now, if only this, if only that . . . it is that way with cricket.

Even with a walking stick in old age the batsmen stop to play the perfect shot in the mirror . . .

'Footfalls echo in the memory
Down the passage we did not take,
Towards the door we never opened
Into the Rose Garden.'

That is the truth of the matter, though I cannot for the life of me recall who T. S. Eliot played for!

12 ...and on to Headingley

ENGLAND

	First innings			Second innings	
J. H. Edrich	c Mallett, b Thomson	62	b Mallett		35
B. Wood	lbw, b Gilmour	9	lbw, b Walker		25
D. S. Steele	c Walker, b Thomson	73	c G. Chappell, b Gilmour		92
J. H. Hampshire	lbw, b Gilmour	14	c G. Chappell, b Thomson		0
K. W. R. Fletcher	c Mallett, b Lillee	8	c G. Chappell, b Lillee		14
*A. W. Greig	run out	51	c & b Mallett		49
†A. P. E. Knott	lbw, b Gilmour	14	c Thomson, b Lillee		31
P. H. Edmonds	not out	13	c sub (Turner), b Gilmour		8
C. M. Old	b Gilmour	5	st Marsh, b Mallett		10
J. A. Snow	c Walters, b Gilmour	0	c Marsh, b Gilmour		9
D. L. Underwood	c G. Chappell, b Gilmour	0	not out		0
Extras	(b 4, lb 15, nb 9, w 11)	39	(b 5, lb 2, w 2, nb 9)		18
		288			**291**

Fall of wickets: 1-25, 2-137, 3-159, 4-189, 5-213, 6-268, 7-269, 8-284, 9-284.

1-55, 2-70, 3-103, 4-197, 5-209, 6-210, 7-272, 8-276, 9-287.

Bowling: Lillee 28-12-53-1, Thomson 22-8-53-2, Gilmour 31.2-10-85-6, Walker 18-4-54-0, I. Chappell 2-0-4-0.
Second innings: Lillee 20-5-48-2, Gilmour 20-5-72-3, Thomson 20-6-67-1, Walker 15-4-36-1, Mallett 19-4-50-3.

AUSTRALIA

	First innings			Second innings	
R. B. McCosker	c Hampshire, b Old	0	not out		95
†R. W. Marsh	b Snow	25	b Underwood		12
*I. M. Chappell	b Edmonds	35	lbw, b Old		62
G. S. Chappell	c Underwood, b Edmonds	13	c Steele, b Edmonds		12
R. Edwards	lbw, b Edmonds	0			

K. D. Walters	lbw, b Edmonds	19	not out	25
G. J. Gilmour	c Greig,			
	b Underwood	6		
M. H. N. Walker	c Old, b Edmonds	0		
J. R. Thomson	c Steele, b Snow	16		
D. K. Lillee	b Snow	11		
A. A. Mallett	not out	1		
Extras (lb 5, w 1, nb 3)		9	(b 4, lb 8, nb 2)	14
		135	3 wkts	220

Fall of wickets: 1-8, 2-53, 3-78, 4-78, 5-81, 1-55, 2-161, 3-174.
6-96, 7-104, 8-107, 9-128.
Bowling: Snow 18.5-7-22-3, Old 11-3-30-1, Greig 3-0-14-0, Wood
5-2-10-0, Underwood 19-12-22-1, Edmonds 20-7-28-5.
Second innings: Old 17-5-61-1, Snow 15-5-21-0, Underwood 15-4-40-1,
Edmonds 17-4-64-1, Greig 9-3-20-0.
Toss won by England.
Umpires: D. J. Constant, A. E. Fagg.
Match abandoned—drawn.

Just like old times up here in Yorkshire! There is talk
again of the County Championship, which other counties
have been enjoying on loan since the breaking-up of that
magnificent Yorkshire team of the sixties. Between 1959
and 1969 they won the title seven times.

In those days if you were not 'pinned like ruddy moth
t'sight screen' by Frederick Sewards Trueman, run-out
from mid-wicket by Don Wilson's left hand, or from
cover point by Ken Taylor's right, or caught in the
gulley after a ricochet from Closey's balding pate at
short square leg, you fell victim of Phil Sharpe's loud
auto-suggestion as you took guard: 'Ah, look who it is.
Another caught Sharpe, bowled Illingworth!' Or, indeed,
you were forced to retire happily because the appeals of
Jim Binks were gradually deafening you. If you survived
all that, and more, then you quite enjoyed playing against
Yorkshire!

The truth is that success against them was much sought
after, especially in front of their generous, but strongly
partisan, hordes. England selectors would give serious
consideration to the claims of anyone who got runs or

wickets against Yorkshire on their own varied pitches because he had done it in the lions' den.

Geoff Boycott's run-getting, uninterrupted by Test Match calls, has given a young side the chance of winning something. When they were down over the past few seasons these youngsters were lashed by Yorkshiremen who should know better. Now the profundities slip from the corner of knowing mouths: 'This Phil Carrick is nay a bad player, tha' knows.' Which is the Yorkshire way of telling you that here is an outstanding prospect.

I learned to respect the name of Yorkshire in the County Cricket world when I was just a ten-year-old. A giant of Glamorgan cricket, Johnny Clay, announced his retirement from the game after we had won the Championship in 1948, but he declared that his long-standing ambition had not been achieved. You might think that that was an England cap, but he already had one of those. The truth was he had never played in a Glamorgan side which had beaten Yorkshire in Yorkshire. There just had not been one.

It is evident at Headingley this week, as ever, that there is no other part of the world where cricket is so much an integral part of life. Sons and fathers play, daughters score, mothers make the teas. Being Yorkshire-born means that you are supposed to know about cricket. Mind you, I once discovered that to be a true all-rounder you have to know your brass bands, too.

Invited to address the Wombwell Cricket Society some years ago, I arrived in the grand metropolis of Barnsley with my team mate, Peter Walker, just before lunch. A plate of Yorkshire pud and gravy later, we were standing on the stage at Wombwell High School talking briefly to the pupils about cricket, but most importantly, judging the instrumental brass competition. A tiny young lad with spectacles won it. He looked so trapped in the middle of this octopus of a euphonium.

'Rather nice,' I remarked to a teacher. 'That lad,

without any physical advantages, has got such a pleasing musical talent.'

'That's best bowler in t'school,' he came back without a smile. From this deep confidence in their own abilities in the game comes a natural conceit. It tests the patience sometimes. For although Yorkshire players in the sixties always sounded as if they were at each other's throats, they were brazenly loyal to each other outside their own dressing rooms.

Everyone thought everyone else should be in the England side. Well, let us be fair, they were frequently right.

Under Ron Burnett they won the championship of 1959. Those of 1960 and 1962 were won under Vic Wilson. He toured Australia, though without playing a Test. The other team members were Sharpe, Padgett, Close, Illingworth, Taylor, Binks, Don Wilson and Trueman—all Test match players. Stott, Bolus, Cowan, Ryan, Platt and Nicholson missed the honour, though Bolus made it with Notts. The wins of 1963, 1966, 1967, 1968 involved two basic changes: Boycott for Stott and Hampshire for Vic Wilson.

To most minds, human personification of Yorkshire self-confidence is best expressed by Fred Trueman in almost all his words and actions.

He once raced in to bowl in a county match at Harrogate. Three successive balls went a yard wide down the leg side.

'Ruddy wicket's nay straight,' he proclaimed. A fourth ball he sent down, again down the leg side.

'Stumps aren't in line, Dusty,' he puffed at umpire Rhodes. 'Fetch ruddy chain out.'

Play was halted. A procession of ground staff followed the umpires out of the groundsman's shed to the middle. The chain was attached from middle stump to middle stump and found perfect. The creases were checked and found plumb. Alas, Fred was geometrically proved wrong.

He took some sweat off his forehead, rubbed it into the new ball, but could not resist an aside to the non-striker as he lumbered back to his mark.

'Ah'll 'ave a fiver with thee son. Summat wrong wi' that ruddy chain, tha' knows.'

Is that not what is meant by the saying 'When Yorkshire is strong, England is strong.' The divine right of the Yorkshireman becomes the divine right of the Englishman and on the international cricket field it has often done us the power of good.

However, for the past six seasons they have not been as good as their word, and their greatest player Geoff Boycott even shuns the three lions. Yet, faith in their home-born players and in themselves was bound sooner or later to see them flutter new wings and fly towards their old nest at the top of the tree.

None of us minds them being there as long as they take the country with them.

Stalemate in the Lord's Test set many talking of the days when leg spin would have winkled 'em out.

No use bleating about the past unless the present can learn a lesson or two from it. Those very few home-grown wrist spinners who have found English first-class cricket a profitable business since the war, and have gone on to play for England, did not remain on the international scene for long. I am thinking of the specialist rather than all-rounders like Freddie Brown and Bob Barber, and excluding the likes of Barrington, Graveney, Fletcher and Hampshire, who have twirled their individual brands of mischief from time to time. I am sure they will not be offended.

Doug Wright, of course, played 34 times for England, but the others did not last as long: Eric Hollies 13 Tests, Roly Jenkins 9, Tommy Greenhough 4, Robin Hobbs 7.

It is commonly said that no team can afford to carry a leg-spinner who cannot bat, but I would wager that Ian Chappell and Tony Greig would have been prepared to select Intikhab Alam for their sides at Lord's and even make the promise that he would not have an innings at all. If his talent is strong enough to stand up as a Test bowler it should not matter whether he can bat or not. Yet this is all hypothetical stuff. At the moment England does not have suitable candidates.

Jim Higgs, Australia's current leg-spinner, is conceding 30 runs to the wicket, but to be fair to him, being a member of a touring party's second string can be frustrating. The Test players relax in county matches and drop catches off the bowling of those straining to break in. This inevitably happens to all touring sides and I do not suppose that these Aussies are exceptions.

If leg-spin is out, perhaps it is possible to conclude about that second Test that the bowling lacked flight, and if that be proven, then it can be remedied.

England's problem is as always: Derek Underwood's style. His flat trajectory poses few problems in the air. On a wicket which is rain-affected, however, or damaged in any serious way, he is a match winner.

On good wickets or bad he is a fine bowler, unlike any other, and a splendid trier. England selectors hate going into a Test match in this country without him. Given our normal share of rain he is an insurance policy. Here at Headingley they will need one. Indeed, in the fifth Test at Adelaide last winter his 7–113 and 4–102 was excellent bowling and throughout the tour his steadiness and accuracy earned him the respect of all.

Many critics insist that he should bowl slower and flight the ball more. Obviously the ball is more inclined to bite and turn if it is thrown higher. Furthermore, the bowler is presenting more problems to the batsmen in the air. It is not just a question of picking up the line and the turn off the wicket, but the flight too. My own feeling is that Derek Underwood is not as happy or at his most effective as a slow, flighty bowler.

His run-up has a pace and rhythm out of which the arm

speed comes naturally, somewhere near medium pace.
Running in at that tempo and holding back the arm
action to send the slower ball does not deceive, indeed
it is almost too obvious for Test-class batsmen. Zaheer,
for example, gave him some brutal treatment, off the
back foot mainly, in Kent's game against Gloucestershire
on a slow turning wicket at Cheltenham College recently.

A bowler such as Bishen Bedi, who has many subtleties
in flight never slows up the arm action. On the contrary,
his deception comes often from a fast-moving arm
sending a quickly revolving ball in a looping trajectory
down the wicket. The high parabola may suggest a slow
speed but, at the batsman's end, the ball gets pace and
extra bounce, the priceless ingredients.

Lesser slow bowlers do not. Mind you, not even Bedi,
Benaud, nor S. F. Barnes himself, bowling with a child's
'power-ball', would have reached bail high at Lord's.

The virtues of flight hardly need emphasising by me.
England's attack, and Australia's too, lacks that important
dimension. It left few options for the captains to set
traps in front of the bat, coaxing the mis-drive short or
long, when a wicket as slow as Lord's has blunted the
fast bowling menace. The role of the spinner has become
simply keeping tight control while the faster men are
taking breath before another new ball.

As far as England is concerned, Tony Greig's adventures in the spin trade have clouded the issue, too. His
efforts are inspired and aggressive, but not of the proper
quality. So should England ignore this extra art of flight
and press on regardless? Personally, I see no point in
playing Australia at their own fast bowling game. To
win the Ashes England have to bowl them out. Thank-
fully the line-up for Headingley this week includes
Edmonds and Underwood, and excludes a batsman.

If seven batsmen are not going to get the runs the
eighth rarely makes the difference, and in any case
Edmonds does open the batting occasionally for Middle-

sex. His bowling is genuinely slow and he can turn the ball sharply. He may be expensive in his first Test match, but his selection is a positive attempt to win the match and go to the Oval for the fourth Test on level terms.

There are other selections which do not appear so sensible, and one is the recall of Keith Fletcher. Fletcher is a cricketer I have always admired, but I honestly believe he is one of those still suffering shell-shock after the tour to Australia. He was dropped, almost illogically, after the first Test at Birmingham, when he worked bravely for a half-century in the second innings on a wet wicket, but asking him to come back now has no cricket logic. Headingley has never been a happy ground for him. There was a period when the Yorkshire crowd believed that their Phil Sharpe should have been in the side and fielding at first slip where he was such an expert. The sight of Fletcher in his place putting down chances only aroused their disapproval, and Yorkshiremen do not keep that sort of feeling quiet. Dennis Amiss is left out this time, as well as Graham Gooch. John Hampshire will bat at number four.

The last of Hampshire's 7 Test matches was in 1972. Coming in for the fifth Test at the Oval he scored 42 and 20. A gifted striker of the ball, he now owes his selection to the fact that his confidence is intact and he could possibly collect runs quickly enough to put England in a winning position. Hendrick and Lever were both chosen, along with Snow and Woolmer, but now, on the day, the first two have been found unfit after injuries sustained for their counties mid-week, and Woolmer stands down for Edmonds. Chris Old gets a recall and for Australia Gary Gilmour replaces Turner. Gilmour, of course, routed England on this very ground in the Prudential Cup competition. He is very much a player of all-round talents and the touring side are stronger for his presence on this particular occasion.

The first day's cricket was what many would recognise

as a typical Headingley day. The ball moved about a
little in the air and more off the pitch. The wicket was
woefully slow, which made the scoring of runs an
unadventurous business too. Greig won the toss and
batted, and by the close of the first day England were
251 for 5, Edrich 62, Steele 73 and Greig not out 46.
Gilmour got a wicket with the new ball, Wood padding
up to an inswinger, but Fletcher's appearance again
managed to bring the worst out of Lillee—or the best,
depending whose side you are on. Mallett obliged with a
catch in the gully and Fletcher was gone.

In spite of Greig's aggression, England were only able
to extend their score to 288. It was difficult to evaluate it.
More evidence was required to say which team held the
advantage. Possibly Gilmour's figures of 6 for 85
indicated that swing bowling would be the most effective,
but when rain stopped play an hour before the official
close on this second day, the game had turned topsy-
turvy. Phil Edmonds stood with glazed look before the
television cameras trying to explain how it felt to have
taken 5 wickets for 17 runs in a Test debut against
Australia. The tourists innings was shattered, though
Thomson and Lillee were still at the crease with Mallett
to come—107 for 8.

It ought to be written first that John Snow had bowled
magnificently, getting movement off the seam, and
finishing with figures of 16 overs, 7 maidens, 1 wicket
for 18 runs and that included the dropping of a straightforward chance from Ian Chappell by Old at third slip.
Marsh had opened the innings in Turner's absence, and
very sensibly he played too, until Snow brought one
back through his backward defence to bowl him.
Edmonds followed Underwood into the attack, the score
77 for 2 and he ran into a belligerent Australian captain
who laid on some hefty sweep shots for singles. Then a
faster ball, extremely short, which had a mid-wicket
boundary written all over it, beat Chappell's pull-shot for

pace—too slow not too fast—and over went his wicket. Edwards, who had jarred his foot in a typical run-saving dive into the boundary boards on the first day, entered with a runner. Neither of them had the trouble of sorting out the calling, because Edwards padded up to his first ball without offering a shot; it came in with the arm, and he was lbw, adding a third nought to the two he managed at Headingley in 1972.

One over remained before tea. Greg Chappell swept the third ball with a crisp ring of the bat. Before the eye could follow, it had been pouched by Underwood at square leg, about twenty yards in from the fence. 81-5 and miracles were happening. Walters played a very similar shot to his captain's to a very similar ball but was lbw not bowled. Walker was drawn forward full stretch by a beauty which pitched, turned and found the edge on the way to Old's hands at slip. Gilmour picked up a short ball from Underwood to be caught at mid-wicket— in the end nothing surprised, all logic was gone.

Phillippe Henri Edmonds, born in Lusaka, Northern Rhodesia, now Zambia, learned his cricket in England at Skinners School and at Cranbrook. He went up to Cambridge and captained the University in 1973. He won a Middlesex cap in 1974 but is still only 24 years old, young for a top-class spinner. I have seen him bowl better than this. He will have a stricter command of length and line and not get anything like the success he had in that first innings at Leeds. Fred Titmus at Lord's has spent long hours trying to persuade him not to try to bowl the unplayable ball every ball. He has many variations which can prove expensive in this class, yet, apart from this note of caution (for his sake), one cannot withhold from him the accolade of a brilliant Test match performance.

On Saturday, the third and crucial day of English advance on their lead of 153, the whole decor at Headingley was tough and cheerless, grey clouds blown by stiff winds overhead: many rows of empty seats and few encouraging roars to support the heroes who had done nothing short of effecting a massive shift in the balance of power between the two countries within two Tests.

There was no underestimating Australia's fighting reserves. Gilmour bowled particularly fast, digging in some short ones which tested out the horsehair in the batting gloves, yet the sobre, sombre ground reflected the run rate of 2 an over. Edrich showed that he was in no mood to repeat the Lord's crawl and tried to get after Mallett. He failed but with the unsettled weather drifting all over Yorkshire, England needed to buy as much time as possible. Greig again answered the call as Steele worked his way steadily to another innings of substance. Around David Steele there has built up a sort of John Bull hero cult—the silver-haired lad of quiet demeanour, spectacles, jockey cap and a stout heart, called to do special duty for his country. He strides to the wicket with the gait of a man with trouble to sort out—like a vicar turned gunfighter.

However, as it was painful to watch the end of Dennis Amiss, so it was to see Keith Fletcher perform his own dance of death. Mallett's first ball to him found the outside edge of the bat and sped quickly at catchable height between Marsh and Ian Chappell. 'That's it, give 'em a chance Fletcher,' came the cat-calls. He prodded and paced about, bemused like an animal wounded. His feet would not move and ball by ball his attackers crowded him. His chief tormenters Lillee and Thomson were recalled.

Bouncers were liberally delivered. In one desperate swing of the bat he attempted to play a sort of Caribbean cover drive off Lillee . . . and missed. It prompted more sharp comment moments later when an announcement called for a car to be moved. 'It can't be Fletcher's anyway. He can't drive.' The crowd was alive now.

Yet, slowly, out of one of the cruellest corners of sporting experience, Fletcher began to emerge. He objected to Turner, 12th man, fielding for the injured Edwards, standing at short leg where he is a specialist. In that small gesture he had briefly taken the battle to the enemy. They were riled, snorted down more bouncers, but at least they knew he was there. For just those few moments before tea, there was just the tiniest platform for his recovery. But it was not to be. Immediately after the break he wafted his bat at Lillee and was magnificently held at second slip.

When Greig arrived at the crease it was a different game. His timing alone sent the ball skimming to the boundaries. Steele plugged on. In one marvellous over of cricket we saw Lillee and Greig at their best. Lillee rushed down the hill and let go a ball which looked to cut back through Greig's guard. He got an inside edge to it. Marsh was beaten by the movement too and England collected four lucky runs. It could easily have been the loss of their captain. Lillee stood half way down the wicket and glared. Greig marched up to him and tapped down a mark on the pitch. Lillee watched and recommended another one a little further over. Greig accepted the advice. Lillee bowled again, Greig stretched forward and played a superb off-drive. As Lillee reached the end of his follow through, Greig held a statuesque pose, his bat still at the end of its arc, pointing at Lillee, as if to say: 'Now don't be facetious or I'll do you again.'

It was a memorable confrontation and was the first time in the match that I felt England knew they were masters of the situation.

It was interesting too that Ashley Mallett, with his low trajectory, did not get the same spin out of the wicket as Edmonds, though his 3 for 50 in 19 overs was useful bowling out of a total of 291. If ever a man deserved a century it was David Steele but he succumbed to Gilmour for 92. Australia were left 445 to win this third Test and so keep the Ashes. Most of history was against them because the highest score ever made to win a Test match in England was 404, yet they might draw strength from the fact that Don Bradman's 1948 Australians were the ones who managed it.

One thing was certain, they would surely not fall as easily the second time. In fact they might, but not to the spin of Edmonds, rather to Snow, who beat the bat so often it was astonishing that he could end up with no wickets for 23 in 15 overs at the close of the fourth day. Rick McCosker entrenched himself. Nothing looked likely to move him or prevent his century coming because he was 95 not out and Australia 220 for 3. All day Tuesday was available to make 225 with 7 wickets standing. One side would surely win. The 21,000 who had watched the drama unfold had seen Ian Chappell in his most determined mood. Edmonds began to be expensive and so did Old. Underwood bowled Marsh to complete 200 wickets in Test cricket, a brilliant achievement, but otherwise could not get the breakthrough. My money, going into the last day, was on Snow making the break and Underwood keeping it tight. The ball turned still, but slowly and lowly, and Edmonds and Greig would have to bowl sparingly.

One of the most famous day's cricket began, or rather, did not begin on that Tuesday, 19th August, at Headingley at 6.50 a.m. when George Cawthray, the Yorkshire County groundsman, rolled back his covers. There he found that the wicket had been damaged. Turf was gouged out in between the creases. A tin of motor oil was found nearby, the contents of which had been poured on to the wicket over the area where the ball usually pitches.

It transpired that while it was dark, saboteurs climbed into the ground, evading the one policeman who was guarding the ground and went to the covered wicket. One or two of them wriggled under the covers and did their damage. Then they painted slogans on the walls outside which revealed their intent. 'George Davis is innocent' they read. 'Free George Davis'. Who, we all asked, is George Davis? His name is not in Wisden but is certain to be there next year.

George Davis turned out to be a prisoner serving a 20-year jail sentence for armed robbery. A ring of his supporters have been claiming for many months that Davis is innocent of the crime. Indeed a campaign to secure his release was launched back in April, a year to the day after the robbery. Already they have rammed a car into the gates of Buckingham Palace and into the doors of the *Daily Telegraph* and other newspapers to draw attention to Davis's case.

All that concerned us that day was that the captains could not find a pitch remotely like the one they had played on. The Test was abandoned and no other game arranged because it was totally impracticable in the time available.

If anything made the cause of George Davis easier to bear it was the arrival of heavy rain in mid-afternoon. It came down hard enough and long enough to have made a draw inevitable. Cricket was the loser, but neither captain could claim to have been 'robbed'.

As I drove back to South Wales I realised how extraordinary this season had been, and I had been as close to the game as any over twenty years.

NO LAUGHTER WHEN THE BADDIES WIN

If someone had written a film script of the events of this cricket season a director would have rejected it and accused the author of trying too hard; squeezing out the drama for effect.

Flying in a cast of eight nations to battle for a World Cup in glorious sunshine day after day for a fortnight is fanciful enough. Like the good 'ole days at the flicks all they did not do in the name of the Pru' was to hang upside down from airborne bi-planes or slip out a routine of formation dances at Lord's.

At this early stage we were not short of goodies and baddies either. Our country's crack shot G. Boycott vowed never again to draw his gun for England and retreated to the hills.

The tall blond Springbok, two-gun Tony Greig loped on to the scene, lead flying from both hands as an obvious threat to the resident sheriff, Mike Denness, who got so giddy spinning round to avoid the snipers that he could scarcely tell head from tails and, when he could, his Birmingham weatherman spoke with forked tongue.

All the action, bounteous and bad, was heaped into a fortnight, Jeff Thomson's first over lasted eleven balls, and a 'Harvey Smith'. How could anything else match that? It did, and got better.

Some rounds the baddies won. Thomson's bouncer knocked down little Mendis from Sri Lanka; but little Kalli from West Indies clouted Dennis Lillee back.

There were run outs, catches, blocks and bangs to send the memory spinning but, at last, when June 21st came, it was time to settle down to a peaceful war, the main feature—'Fight for the Ashes'. Yes, this was one the film director would like.

Sudden defeat at Edgbaston, then the fight back, gradual but bearing all the nuances of character; ball by ball, over by over, the drama built up without a jerk or an action out of place.

'Yes. I was enjoying that,' the film director might say.

'Good stuff. Make an epic. But now what are you trying to sell me? Someone digging up the pitch? Don't be daft. That wouldn't happen. Just let the action talk for itself, my boy, I don't want impossibilities.'

It is easy to joke at the truth but impossible to laugh at it. Cricket has yet again been found vulnerable. So it was when demonstrators vented their hatred of South African politics on the sports lovers of the country. They forced cricket administrators to rush off to find out the most unlikely information—the cost of rolling barbed wire around the boundary, of hiring hundreds of police and guard dogs, of taking all the precautions that should be foreign to sport.

Again this week in a silly singular week, minority vandalism wins. Few would discredit a just cause. If G. Davis should be outside, not inside, Her Majesty's Prison for the next 20 years, it is above all the concern of the courts and those who know for certain he is innocent or guilty. What concerns the cricket world is that repeated vulnerability.

For Davis's brother-in-law to say that cricket is not important is far from the truth. In an odd sort of way he has paid the game a compliment. His cause has been best served by interfering with a sporting institution which is an integral part of English life. Too late now.

So, lest we take ourselves too seriously, it is worth recalling other days when wickets were tampered with and how the shocking incidents became the best remembered stories—in my county anyway.

Who would worry about security these days if Frank Ryan of Hants and Glamorgan was still playing? A beautiful left arm spinner of the '20s, Ryan carried his affection for the gay life to the point of eccentricity. Rolling back the covers for a county match one morning a groundsman disturbed the slumbering Ryan, a relic from a pavilion party, but revived him with hot tea before play began.

Or, how the Notts team, enjoying many pints of beer in the Grand Hotel opposite Cardiff Arms Park in the '30s climbed the wall of the ground, ran to the pitch, sought midnight relief over the wicket and ran back to cover. Next day against Larwood and Voce on a 'wet' wicket Turnbull scored a double century and Dai Davies one.

Ah well. Only once it happened to me, in 1964, that

vandals did damage overnight. Huge letters painted in thick red paint the length of the wicket announced that Rag Week had come to . . . yes, you can guess—Heading-ley.

We agreed to play on if they mowed it a little and painted the red letters green. They did that. We were roundly commended for our sportsmanship by all, but, in defence of Ian Chappell who did not wish to continue this Third Test in unusual conditions, I should mention that we lost the game by an innings.

13 *The Oval—Fourth and Final Test*

AUSTRALIA

R. B. McCosker	c Roope, b Old	127	not out	25
A. Turner	c Steele, b Old	2	c Woolmer, b Greig	8
*I. M. Chappell	c Greig, b Woolmer	192		
G. S. Chappell	c Knott, b Old	0	not out	4
R. Edwards	c Edrich, b Snow	44	c Old, b Underwood	2
K. D. Walters	b Underwood	65		
†R. W. Marsh	c & b Greig	32		
M. H. N. Walker	c Steele, b Greig	13		
J. R. Thomson	c Old, b Greig	0		
D. K. Lillee	not out	28		
A. A. Mallett	not out	5		
Extras (lb 5, w 2, nb 17)		24	(lb 1)	1

9 wkts dec 532   2 wkts 40

Fall of wickets: 1-7, 2-284, 3-286, 4-356, 5-396,   1-22, 2-33.
6-441, 7-477, 8-477, 9-501.

Bowling: Old 28-7-74-3, Snow 27-4-74-1, Woolmer 18-3-38-1, Edmonds 38-7-118-0, Underwood 44-13-96-1, Greig 24-5-107-3, Steele 2-1-1-0.
Second innings: Old 2-0-7-0, Snow 2-0-4-0, Edmonds 6.1-2-14-0, Greig 5-2-9-1, Underwood 2-0-5-1.

ENGLAND

B. Wood	b Walker	32	lbw, b Thomson	22
J. H. Edrich	lbw, b Walker	12	b Lillee	96
D. S. Steele	b Lillee	39	c Marsh, b Lillee	66
G. R. J. Roope	c Turner, b Walker	0	b Lillee	77
R. A. Woolmer	c Mallett, b Thomson	5	lbw, b Walters	149
*A. W. Greig	c Marsh, b Lillee	17	c Marsh, b Lillee	15
†A. P. E. Knott	lbw, b Walker	9	c Marsh, b Walters	64
P. H. Edmonds	c Marsh, b Thomson	4	run out	7

154

C. M. Old	not out	25	c I. Chappell, b Walters		0
J. A. Snow	c G. Chappell, b Thomson	30	c & b Walters		0
D. L. Underwood	c G. Chappell, b Thomson	0	not out		3
Extras (lb 3, w 3, nb 12)		18	(b 2, lb 15, w 5, nb 17)		39
		191			538

Fall of wickets: 1-48, 2-78, 3-83, 4-96, 5-103, 6-125, 7-131, 8-147, 9-190.

1-77, 2-202, 3-209, 4-331, 5-371, 6-522, 7-522, 8-533, 9-533.

Bowling: Lillee 19-7-44-2, Thomson 22.1-7-50-4, Walker 25-7-63-4, Mallett 3-1-16-0.

Second innings: Lillee 52-18-91-4, Thomson 30-9-63-1, Mallett 64-31-95-0, Walker 46-15-91-0, I. Chappell 17-6-52-0, Walters 10.5-3-34-4, G. Chappell 12-2-53-0, Edwards 2-0-20-0.

Umpires: H. D. Bird, T. W. Spencer.

Toss won by Australia.

Match drawn.

There was always the likelihood in hot sunshine at the Oval that the toss for the fourth and final Test would be important. Wickets at the Oval have been slow and safe for batting, with some turn, but nothing hostile enough to frighten Test match players. Ian Chappell was lucky this time and in a single day's cricket it was possible to say that even with the extra sixth day to play, this would be an Australian win or a draw.

Alan Turner replaced Gilmour in the Australian side. Gilmour had taken 9 wickets at Headingley, so it meant that whatever problems might arise in bowling out England, Chappell was determined not to be short of runs. Not that Turner contributed. He was caught at backward short leg by Steele off Old. One wicket was down for seven, and I heard whisperings of another Australian collapse. That was the only wicket to fall on that first day!

McCosker and Ian Chappell battled through many mistimings in the morning and expanded their ambitions as the warm day and the wicket took its toll of the

England bowlers. In England's side Graham Roope, recently in very good form for Surrey, replaced Keith Fletcher and Woolmer returned instead of Hampshire. The side bristled with bowlers, nine in all, and expert close fielders. Greig's problem by late afternoon was getting these fielders into positions where they mattered.

McCosker has been more impressive as the tour has gone on. There have been a lot of words written and spoken about his tendency to play across to leg, but in this innings his technique was watertight. He does not score many runs in the classic arc between mid-off and square cover, but he cuts vigorously. His defensive work was all with a straight bat and he extended this often to send straight drives fizzing past the bowlers. His great strength through mid-wicket does not necessarily mean that he is weak in defence around off-stump. True this is only a slow wicket, but presumably he has scored most of his runs on faster Australian pitches. He was 57 when he failed to get on top of a cut at Edmonds but Roope, usually the most safe and agile slip fielder, dropped the chance. Underwood was the unfortunate bowler. After that he took no risks and reached that first Test hundred which the vandals at Headingley had taken away from him by digging up the pitch on the last morning when he was 95 not out. With 74 on the board he had become the first Australian batsman to reach 1,000 runs on the tour.

Ian Chappell batted for seven and three-quarter hours and was out to his first chance for 192, just four short of his Test match best—196 against Pakistan at Adelaide. He is a curious mixture of fidgety nerves and lissome strokes. When he is at the crease he fiddles about with his cap, collar, cuff, bat, box almost everything in quick succession; he even moves forward to a ball before finally going back, or vice-versa, but when he puts bat to ball, it is graceful and beautifully timed. He is a fine judge too of what shots are 'on' and what are not, and that is a rare asset for a player who is happiest when he is 'getting after' the bowling. Incredibly, when he was out, having afforded so many people so much cricketing pleasure, he did so in a huff. I am not certain whether he was annoyed with himself for holing out at that particular stage to a long-hop. The crowd rose to him, applauded him from the middle, yet he refused to acknowledge his reception—not even a nod. Australian journalists in the Press Box could not excuse him. To me it was a classic case of a cricketer getting too close to his sport. Ian Chappell would hate to be associated with anything that smacked of an accepted courtesy; formalities freeze him. Whatever was passing through his mind, and accepting that he does not carry a book of etiquette around with him, this was a myopic, ungenerous reaction to good-will.

Someone who responded quite differently was Ross Edwards, who announced his retirement from Test cricket during the game. He was given the honour of leading Australia into the field, to a fine reception, but first he was to contribute 44 runs to a massive 532 for 9 declared.

The third day, Saturday, was near purgatory for England. Bad light eventually stopped play, but not before we had seen Max Walker at his best. England were reduced to 169 for 8 and all day they suffered Australia's special brand of torture, the slow drip of acid fast bowling gradually eroding confidence and frustrating efforts to score. The victims simply scratched around until the death blow came. Steele, once again, battled out the issues but Lillee bowled him through his legs as his weight leaned across to the off. Roope got nought, an unlucky comeback; all England could do was to curse the bad luck which had them off and on the field for poor light.

Jeff Thomson appeared to bowl much faster in this match than any other. His run-up looks longer, his paces are wider and his rhythm more natural. Hitherto he almost jogged in and looked for speed from his coil-spring action. Lillee was magnificent, but the wicket beat them all.

There surely was no way out for Greig's side. 341 behind and following on. Yet they launched a rearguard action, slow, resolute and quite without consideration of squaring the series. Progress was almost too slow to bear. Suffice it to say that Edrich did his bit in inimitable style, Steele too, and then Roope and Woolmer occupied most of the fourth day with a stand of 122 in 3 hours and 40 minutes. Roope was the more aggressive partner and he was unfortunate to be out just five minutes before fading light took the players off the field once more. Mallett toiled without much turn or success and it became clearer and clearer that England at least were going to have the satisfaction of sending the tourists home with sore feet. Woolmer for example collected just two singles in an hour before tea.

The final day was still an attritious war and England's score in an innings of 13½ hours had reached 538. Woolmer to his eternal credit and playing to orders got a maiden hundred, 149. He and Roope did nobly, because they were under great pressures from the nervous start, right to the end. Woolmer now has the mixed distinction of having scored the slowest hundred against Australia, 6 hours and 35 minutes.

A lot had happened in six days and yet nothing had. Perhaps more than anything it was pleasing to see the Oval brimming with spectators. It is such a plain, mournful place when it is empty. And there was always Harold 'Dickie' Bird, a rare character if there ever was one.

In fact the Oval changes little—a large hard ground, often daunting to fielders, and England have had two days of it. In a hot dry August it is like tramping over a desert of broken egg shells in bare feet. Breezes drift off the Thames wafting thick brewery smells up the nostrils, malt settles on the tongue, reviving or revolting as the fieldsman's taste may be.

Up in his pavilion eyrie the old leader Stuart Surridge watches over his old empire with patrician eye, looking still fresh and fit as if, like Napoleon, he lurks in the hills awaiting the recall to arms.

Ken Barrington, now a nervous selector, gives putting lessons to friends in the Long Room rather than see England struggle. Announcements boom out as ever on Surrey's ground in nasal military tones as if the order not to leave litter at the close of play is an extract from Queen's Regulations. Wet or fine, any day of the week, John Edrich is usually batting.

Occasionally the cast changes and, in this Test match, it is impossible to keep umpire Harold Bird out of the action for long. A kindly soul, cricket his love, justice his chief intent and, so that you can weigh his responsibilities, he acts the Lord High Executioner with enough pomp to win him life membership of the G. and S. Society.

He makes 'opera comique' of a serious job. Some do not approve: others like me are happy to smile at him as long as he enjoys the confidence of the players, and that he obviously does or they would not have him there at all.

In Australia he has become something of a national favourite through the medium of television. His mannerisms have caught on. He has an academic stoop, surprising for one so young in the trade—just 42 years old.

As bowlers run in behind him his hands go down to the hem of his white coat and hoists it up, like Grandad going for a paddle in the sea. Run outs never surprise him because, even when no runs are on, he launches himself conspicuously into all the likely vantage spots. To do this he back pedals violently from the stumps at the bowler's end crouching and fixing the crease with an iron stare.

He is one of the few umpires who can successfully communicate with the club secretary from the middle of the pitch. On Thursday his heavy Yorkshire voice easily infiltrated the pavilion stonework and, in seconds, the military man was commanding spectators to sit still behind the bowler's arm.

The same voice announces 'no balls' with a long baritone glissando descending even after the applause has died down into the dark brown regions of the bass clef. He signals the widest wides ever seen.

His many other attitudes—the flexing of his arms inside rolled up sleeves, the hands placed in the middle of his back, the staring eyes, flat white hat and stentorian northern tones have been most likely acquired from one of the greatest umpiring characters, Alec Skelding.

'That concludes the entertainment for today' Alec would announce for thousands to hear and march off in his white boots which were unique in those days.

Having downed a few pints in his favourite Leicester pub one night, Alec took his leave, eyes atwinkling, arms flexing, theatrical as ever. He bade everyone an individual goodnight, opened the door, went through waving and closed it. Everyone knew, except him, that he had walked into the telephone booth.

Out he came ' 'Ave just up'eld an appeal against the light, gentlemen,' he announced loudly. 'Ee, it's ruddy dark in there. They'll not play any more in there today, y'know.'

Bird may be the imitator and he has his critics. The belief is that the best adjudicators control the game quietly. He has no right to expect so much from a non-talking part, however central it is. All that concerns the players is that he is sound in justice.

Long hours of concentration make umpiring a tough job. They all do it because they love the game and, if Dickie Bird wants us to see how meticulous he is or Tom Spencer how firm he can be or David Constant how

With an unrecognisable stroke David Steele reasserts—'They shall not pass'

Jeff Thomson and umpire Dickie Bird (never known to miss his cue) in operatic form

diligent he can be, then I do not see that we should begrudge them a little licence.

Bobby Simpson always said about slip fielding that he would try to relax between every ball because concentration wore him down. Ian Chappell has taken spells in the outfield for the same reason.

How much harder it is for umpires, and all you will see in Wisden to mark their efforts ball by ball and day by day is 'Bird H. D. (Yorks. and Leics.) First class umpire page 1116. Test panel page 1115.'

Not too glamorous a write-up when you come to think of it.

14   Now the Tests are over

A great deal happened to England's cricket during the four Test match series against Australia; most of it well thought out, some of it not so well.

I am afraid the selectors have to put up with judgments like this, made with hindsight in the way that Mike Denness at Edgbaston was going to emerge as the 'Brain of Britain', or 'Some Mothers do 'ave 'em' in television parlance.

Still, let me voice the inexcusable. First, there was no cricketing argument which justified the recall of Keith Fletcher, especially at Headingley. It is said that Fletcher himself was surprised to be chosen, although he felt his half century on a rain affected wicket in the decisive first Test might have merited selection for the second—for which he was dropped.

Sadly, Fletcher, like Amiss and Denness himself, laboured meekly in the shadow of the devils they knew, which were worse by far than the devil they might not have known. Headingley has never been a happy ground for Fletcher. Old ghosts leapt out to meet him, slip catches tumbled down, and his bat moved involuntarily in hopeful prods and swishes.

The second mistake, at the Oval, completely understandable but nonetheless avoidable, was made by the captain—if he will excuse the impertinence of one who would have been only too delighted to make a draw at all in his place.

The importance of a need for advice from experienced onlookers like Bedser, Hutton, Barrington and Elliot was underlined. This was in the second innings of the last Test at the Oval when Greig allowed Roope and Woolmer to start their innings together. He should have gone in himself, not to attack, but just to pour some English optimism on Australian fires.

Roope, on a pair and Woolmer, inexperienced in Tests, brought the game to a dead stop. Just consider how marginally England's run rate had to be increased over the 13-hour innings, in order to test Australia with a target of over 200 runs on the final afternoon. It was the only way to square the series, even though it required Herculean efforts just to draw.

Australia made mistakes too. Gary Gilmour should have opened the bowling. Wood's errors against him at Headingley, Steele's habit of placing his foot in line with the ball instead of inside the line, all made Gilmour a greater threat than Walker and Thomson.

Ian Chappell stuck too slavishly to his formula. Even without Gilmour, Walker not Thomson should have taken the new ball. Indeed Ian Chappell might have bowled himself much more often especially to those up the order—Edrich, Wood and Steele.

Spin bowling was the last thought in his strategy and he rather over-estimated the power of Lillee, Thomson and Walker to transfix the fresh minds brought into the England side to cure the winter rot. It is a luxury to talk in these terms, especially of England, when all we faced was a prospective hammering.

There were important characters, Greig, not the least, as well as Edrich, Steele and Knott, because it was not only the defence against Australian pace that was required but also runs off the bat and these four did us proud.

Greig's captaincy and a few new faces clearly changed the mentality of the side. Optimism and determination saw batsmen on the front foot instead of lurking apprehensively on the back. Nowhere was this more important than in the first three of the batting order.

Ian Chappell has retired from the Australian captaincy after leading in a record 30 Test matches beginning with the last of the 1970–71 series in which England won the Ashes. Few captains ever enjoy the support of their teams to the extent that Chappell was almost hero worshipped by his.

In many ways he was the thief to catch the thieves. In these days when players push to control every decision made by the management he was their ideal negotiator. In terms of social functions, accepted or refused, courtesies observed or ignored, he and the team certainly gave vent to their feelings.

On the field Chappell and his side are known to players for the many crudities which spurted out of sour mouths. Off the field many of them, the captain especially, have won a legion of friends.

That is the way of their competition; this is the nature of England's enemy and Chappell was always sportsman enough to share a beer at the end of a day and was never arrogant in victory. Under him, Australian cricket has prospered on the field.

Of course, it is easy to have the devotion of your team when you are a winning side. And Chappell was fortunate to be in office when great fast bowling was available. Yet he never had to prove his own credentials as a player of hard defence and vigorous attacking shots, a superb slip fielder and a bowler of more than passing skill—a formidable opponent indeed.

15 John Murray

This summer, May 31st to be exact, John Murray passed the world record for wicket-keeping dismissals when he caught Dudley Owen-Thomas of Surrey off the bowling of Tim Lamb. This was his 1494th victim and the record he overtook was held by Herbert Strudwick. In September Murray retired.

As a young lad in North Kensington, John Murray turned his hand to many sports and was pleased to have a trial at Lord's as a batsman-cum-bowler. Yet he was playing in the final of a Boys' Clubs competition when his wicket-keeper broke a finger and 'J.T.' took over. It was still as a batsman that he was taken on the Lord's ground staff in 1950, but Archie Fowler, the head coach, had him 'keeping straight away, and progress was so fast that two years later he had deputised for the injured Leslie Compton at Leicester. There followed two years in a powerful Royal Air Force side, and at the end of 1955 he took over from Compton, the following year winning his cap. Since then he has been an automatic choice for Middlesex as well as an England Test cricketer twenty-one times.

In that long career, achievements have heaped up and there will be those who recall his century against the West Indies at the Oval in the fifth Test of 1966 with special relish. Never before in Test cricket had the last three wickets produced as much as 361 runs, nor had the last three men scored one hundred and two fifties. 'J.T.' was lbw bowled Sobers 112; Ken Higgs caught and bowled Holford 63; and John Snow not out 59.

Though it was Murray's partnership with Graveney that I remember most. (Perhaps I should mention that I was twelfth man and pretty close to the action.)

The West Indies were three Tests up, one drawn, and there was nothing to salvage for England save some pride. Tom Graveney had played magnificently through the series and in this Test scored 165. Graveney and Murray at the crease together for hours made the most aesthetic sight imaginable.

Murray struck me as one of the rare people I had seen who could make the hooking of a fast bouncer truly elegant. Wes Hall and Charlie Griffith thundered in, but he pivoted with the balance of an ice skater and wafted the ball powerfully away to leg. His drives off the front foot were taken out of the MCC coaching manual, sideways on, left foot right to the pitch of the ball, and the follow-through generous. His wicket keeping has always been stylish, and there is no doubt that he makes a conscious effort to preserve that feeling in all his movements. As a bowler runs into bowl 'J.T.' is synchronised to touch fingertips, and raise both hands to the peak of his cap. Then as he adopts the crouching position his gloves are meticulously placed together, open for inspection, just touching the floor, his balance like a gymnast's. He always claimed to model his art on the talents of Wally Grout. 'I felt as I watched him,' confessed Murray, 'that here was the perfect pair of hands. I felt I wanted to keep wicket like him. He read the game so well, positionally right, you know, never diving unless he was going for a catch.'

After collecting a ball there comes the daily chore of lobbing it back to the bowler or to a fielder. Murray makes of this one of the minieature delights of physical movement. The body bends slightly to make room for a long, languid swinging arm. He truly cares about such things.

There are very few batsmen who played over the last

twenty years who were not caught Murray bowled
Titmus at some time or other. They were complimentary
characters. Almost without a sign to each other, Fred
could feed 'J.T.'s' stumping skills by firing a ball quickly
down the leg side, at almost yorker length. Then there
was the drifter, floating away to the slips. He was very
much part of the success of Fred Titmus.

On tour he has been a marvellous cheerful companion
in spite of the bad luck of being reserve more often than
in the Test side. He was blocked mainly by the Selectors'
preference for Jim Parks who could bat and also keep, in
that order. It is a policy easy to decry now, but J.T.
would be the first to point out that Jim did many fine
things for England behind the stumps and in front of
them.

I recall his humour as the Commonwealth side of 1968
battled with an odd-looking meal in our residence, the
Public Works Department Rest House, Sargodha, in
Pakistan. Every waiter or bearer all over the world he
called 'George'. Coming in to dinner he saw everyone
struggling with the sight and the smell of an unusual
looking chicken curry; everyone except John Hampshire
that is, who insisted it was good stuff. One sniff was
enough for 'J.T.'.

'Don't worry lads,' he said, marching into the kitchen.
We could hear his voice, slow, deliberate and very
London saying, 'Now, George, look here. These are the
eggs; you crack 'em open like this . . . and fry them . . .
like that. Now don't go away George, look here. These
are the potatoes . . . peel 'em, slice 'em, fry 'em too . . . egg
and chips George. O.K., gelde, gelde. Oh, and George,
every meal the same.'

Johnny Hampshire left the field the next day in much
haste, returning two days later about two stone lighter!

John Murray came up the hard way. Young lads on
the Lord's ground staff in his day laboured at the very
bottom of a strict hierarchy. They sold scorecards, swept

stands, bowled to members or pulled the vast heavy roller. Could he have imagined then how his career would end? Lord's packed out, the Gillette Cup Final, Middlesex against Lancashire, and a standing ovation as he made his way for the last time from the Long Room to the middle. The cheers must have been heard in those dark recesses of Lord's where scorecards are churned out on clanking machines, where brooms are kept and boots repaired and, without seeing, all recognised the departure of one of their favourite sons.

Twenty years of endeavour, success and disappointment must have welled up inside him, but perfectly dressed, smartly walking, he raised his bat with certainty and yes—style, and even as Lancashire were hammering home their victory later in the day, and the prize was lost, 'J.T.' was as ever fingertipping his peak, fingertipping his fingertips . . . crouching . . . waiting . . . his very soul ticking with the rhythm of the wicket-keeping art.

16   Lloyd's True Blade

MIDDLESEX
M. J. Smith	b Lever	12
J. M. Brearley	lbw, b Lever	16
C. T. Radley	lbw, b Ratcliffe	15
N. G. Featherstone	c Simmons, b Lee	0
H. A. Gomes	b Ratcliffe	44
G. D. Barlow	c Kennedy, b Ratcliffe	22
J. T. Murray	b Lee	13
P. H. Edmonds	c Ratcliffe, b Lee	29
F. J. Titmus	not out	8
T. M. Lamb	not out	11
Extras (b 2, lb 3, nb 5)		10

Total (8 wkts)   180

Overs: 60.
Did not bat: M. W. W. Selvey.
Fall of wickets: 1-29, 2-32, 3-33, 4-64, 5-114, 6-117, 7-160, 8-160.
Bowling: Lever 12-2-47-2, Lee 12-1-38-3, Ratcliffe 12-5-25-3, Simmons 11-1-32-0, C. Lloyd 1-0-4-0, Wood 12-3-24-0.

LANCASHIRE
B. Wood	b Selvey	13
A. Kennedy	c Radley, b Edmonds	51
F. C. Hayes	c Murray, b Gomes	17
C. H. Lloyd	not out	73
D. Lloyd	not out	22
Extras (b 5, lb 1)		6

Total (3 wkts)   182

Overs: 57.
Did not bat: F. M. Engineer, D. P. Hughes, J. Simmons, R. M. Ratcliffe, P. Lever, P. Lee.
Fall of wickets: 1-26, 2-55, 3-133.
Bowling: Selvey 12-3-21-1, Lamb 9-1-46-0, Titmus 12-4-28-0, Gomes 12-2-39-1, Edmonds 11-1-37-1, Featherstone 1-0-5-0.
Umpires: H. D. Bird, J. G. Langridge.

Lancashire, the favourites, won the Gillette Cup for the fourth time since the competition began in 1963, though there were times when they trod a sticky path in pursuit of Middlesex's 180. The winning runs came with three overs to go.

Cleverly as Middlesex schemed, switched bowlers and fielded with the utmost dedication to their uphill task, there was no way in which they could stem the runs flowing from Clive Lloyd's bat. He went in when the score was 55 for two in the 30th over and only near the end did he need to chance the more ambitious shots. The truth was that Lancashire always had wickets in hand.

Lancashire put Middlesex in to bat first, slightly unorthodox tactics when you think of Gillette Cup matches which have ended in poor light. Yet it was understandable this time because the new start of 10.30 grabbed an extra half hour of bright sunshine in the morning.

It was a disappointment to Middlesex that John Price had to withdraw because of a strained shoulder. He has been a steadying force in the Middlesex attack this summer in one-day cricket, if not quite building up the pace of his best days as an England opener. Lamb replaced him.

It was incredible to be queueing up again at the Lord's car-park on yet another sunny morning for yet another death or glory spectacular played before a full house. Quite a year.

Lancashire, too, in their fifth final, were appearing almost like resident artistes. The only scent of romance in the air was the presence of Middlesex, their first Gillette final, Cinderellas at the ball. How long would it be before their coach changed back to a pumpkin? How long could they extend Lancashire, the accredited experts at the short game?

No finer tribute can be paid Mike Brearley and his side than to say they have got to the final of the Benson and Hedges Cup and now the Gillette Cup with a side scarcely equipped for the job.

They began their innings with confidence full of short singles and with the ball generally meeting the middle of the bat.

Brearley was soon caught on the back foot when he might have survived on the front, a ball from Lever which obviously darted into his pads from outside the off-stump. The score was only 29 and worse was to follow at 32. Lever struck again by bowling Smith off the inside edge of the bat. Gloomy stuff for Middlesex, right against their quiet, but heart-felt optimism, yet exactly what the pundits predicted.

Lever is a most difficult bowler to dominate. Critics may say that he runs in almost faster than he bowls, but the ball has a nasty habit of arriving just short of a length, on the seam, and on or about the off-stump.

Lee, too, has been a prolific wicket-taker since he moved from Northants and he got the wicket of Featherstone splendidly caught at second slip by Simmons.

Gomes and Radley figured in a durable partnership and they showed signs of repelling the ball and tickling a few useful runs to Lancashire's discomfort. Gomes mis-timed many of his drives, but Radley kept him scampering up and down the pitch as if life depended on it. Radley was hit on the back leg and adjudged lbw from the last ball before lunch and a modest Middlesex total was expected. Barlow and Edmonds, with a fine flourish, helped it to more optimistic proportions, but it seemed no great challenge to Lancashire at the end of 60 overs.

Yet all the cruelty of the contest was tossed aside for a few nostalgic moments as John Murray walked to the crease for the last time in his career. No need for the announcer to identify him—the ovation signalled a special occasion.

For all who played against him, he leaves an aura of

elegance, fair play and humour. I laugh to think of him being held up by Customs officers in Karachi as we arrived for a Commonwealth tour in 1968. They were fussing about, inspecting a small package of his which they opened and laid out. About 10 different electric plugs for power points were displayed for all to see—suspicious indeed. In his other hand he carried the team's record player and he kept protesting that these unusual appliances were not criminal equipment; it was simply that, in his experience, electricity tended to come out of some strange holes in the wall in Pakistan! They were not amused.

Lord's stood to him on the way out and in—and Lancashire joined in.

Lancashire appeared to make no headway at all in pursuit of Middlesex's 180 until Clive Lloyd came to the wicket when the score was 55 for 2, Wood and Hayes having gone cheaply.

He helped to carry young Kennedy along at a faster rate and despite a grim grey light, these two broke the defensive cordon which had threatened to stifle their chances.

Titmus bowled his 12 overs for 28 runs. The light faded; shotmaking did not come easily and there were 100 runs to get in 22 overs. Middlesex's fielding was as brilliant as anything seen this season.

Yet Mike Smith dropped Clive Lloyd off Titmus at mid-on, an awkward one to pick out of the crowd, but crucial nonetheless. Lloyd was just eight then, and poor Smith had to retreat to the third man boundary at the Tavern to meet jeers and a banner advising him 'Red Roses Grow on You'.

Lloyd accelerated, took his singles, and hit Lamb over mid-on. The Lancashire throats were loosened, 'Easy, easy'.

Kennedy eventually fell, caught at mid-wicket. Brearley tried allowing Clive Lloyd the single, but the other

The captain's pain . . .

and his pleasure

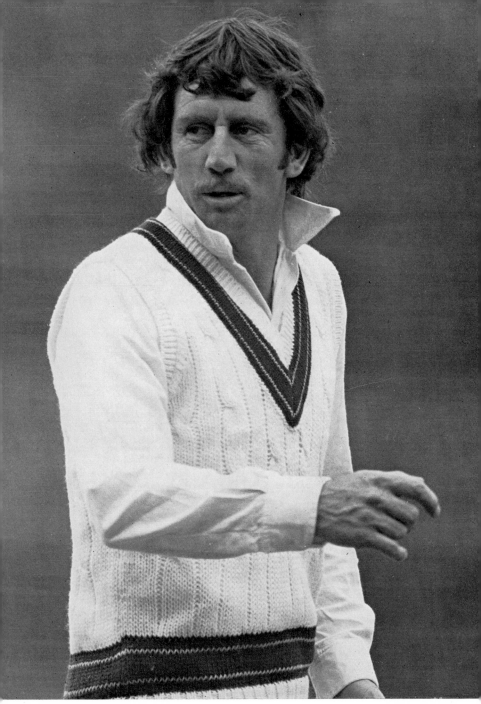

Ian Chappell

Roger Tolchard fends-off a ball from Andy Roberts and Leicestershire hold off Hampshire's challenge for the 1975 County Championship

Lloyd, David the captain, proved too good to be confined. Thirty-two runs were required off the last eight overs, but Middlesex appeared more and more to be bowling half volleys directly at the meat of Clive Lloyd's bat—an exaggeration, but that was the size of his superiority.

17   A Summer of Cricket

Of all the competitions, the one the professional players most want to win is the County Championship. Although it has been severely truncated, now 20 matches instead of 28 as it was in the fifties, it still proves in most minds that the best side of the season ends on top. Personally I would not argue that too strongly in this particular season. The Prudential Cup and the Tests have taken important players away from sides at crucial moments. For example Leicestershire, the ultimate winners, beat Kent who were without Asif Iqbal, Alan Knott, Bob Woolmer and Derek Underwood. Yet, year after year, the side which wins the Championship beats eleven or twelve sides, which is a splendid record.

There is a fine romance about Leicestershire's success. It is a county sparsely populated; interest is hard to drum up, and a casual study of recent history will trace the improvements on the playing field to Michael Turner, the secretary. Turner was a leg-spinner on the county staff who did not make the top class, but enough of the game's spirit entered his veins to enable him to recognise skill and temperament when he saw it. The offer of the captaincy to Tony Lock was one of the brilliant conceptions of post-war cricket. Lock or 'Beau', as he was familiarly known in the playing fraternity, was never anyone's idea of a captain. In the fifties when most captains were amateurs he was thought of as a rather talkative confidence trickster who had got away with throwing his left-arm spinners at the Oval until they declared his action illegal. At Leicestershire he revelled in the authority. His ability was respected by the players and soon his judgement was too. Instead of trailing off and on fields with the smile of the defeated, Leicestershire were suddenly at your throats.

Before I write further I should take care to point out that I am not trying to belittle what went before. My first ever county game was against Leicestershire at Cardiff in 1955. A tough-looking Australian by the name of Jack Walsh trapped me lbw first ball. Charles Palmer captained and Mike Smith, latterly of Warwickshire, was in the side. They played good cricket, talented in many ways, but not winning cricket.

In time with the revival was the move to Grace Road. The ground was new, chilly and without history. Enough has happened there over the past ten years to make the supporters' club bar rattle with talk of success in the Benson and Hedges Cup (they were the first winners), the Gillette Cup and John Player League.

The County Championship however was a special challenge. It had never been won by Leicestershire. Mike Turner aided by his devoted President Mr William Bentley and a forward thinking committee realised that players had to be imported and some of their acquisitions were cleverly thought out. First they detected skills in players who were not finding room to express themselves in other counties. The Yorkshiremen Chris Balderstone, Jack Birkenshaw and Ray Illingworth provide a nucleus. Of course Illingworth was an established player who took his benefit with Yorkshire, yet he was never a captain in his home county. With Leicestershire he captained England. Jack Birkenshaw too became an England player while at Grace Road. Illingworth like Ken Higgs, also an England bowler, fell out with his county. At one time that did not make them terribly popular men on the county circuit. Nowadays the contrary almost holds good. They made their protest against what they saw as unfair treatment. Norman

McVicker, formerly of Warwickshire, falls into the category of one whose play benefited from a change of county, rather like Mick Norman who was once with Northants. From Devon came the Tolchards, Jeff and Roger. Roger is a particularly fine batsman under pressure and a good wicket-keeper though not an exceptional one. If you consider that Peter Booth is from Yorkshire, Barry Dudleston from Cheshire and David Gower from Kent, that leaves two other key men both from overseas, Graham McKenzie, the Australian Test bowler, and Brian Davison from Rhodesia. Quite a medley. It must have appeared a fast-moving world to Terry Spencer the Leicester-born fast bowler, whose splendid career stretched from 1952 to this 1975 season.

During the season I watched Ray Illingworth's men win matches in the obvious but elusive fashion—by scoring their runs quickly and being able to offer swing, speed, spin or seam bowling according to the conditions. The pitches at Grace Road turned enough for their four spinners, Illingworth and Birkenshaw the off-spinners, and Balderstone and Steele the left-armers, to winkle out the toughest opposition.

I was with them in the Station Hotel in Chesterfield, an unlikely place to end a season, on September 13th as they went into their final match. Lancashire, their pursuers, were playing against Sussex at Hove and if the Lancastrians were to take maximum points (18) from that match, Leicestershire would need a minimum of 7 from this tussle with Derbyshire.

They were struck by the mental agonies and physical weaknesses which afflict every side straining for the most coveted prize. Leicestershire supporters bustled up from the railway station that morning, and entered the lovely Queen's Park ground in bright morning sunshine to the news that Illingworth had won the toss. He batted of course. The banners waved—'Leicestershire, Kings of Cricket'. A couple of hours later they were 77 for 6!

The ball moved around in the air and off the wicket and it was only by resolute effort down the bottom of the order, particularly by Jack Birkenshaw, Jeff Tolchard, Graham McKenzie, Norman McVicker and Ken Higgs that two batting bonus points were taken. However the twists of that topsy-turvy day were soon forgotten as Lancashire began to struggle down at Hove. They failed to get maximum points, or even win at all, and the table ended thus:

Leicestershire	12 wins	240 points
Yorkshire	10 wins	224 points
Hampshire	10 wins	223 points
Lancashire	9 wins	219 points

The John Player League title went to Worcestershire though there has been trouble in that camp. The Players' Association had to intervene in a dispute between players and committee half way through the season and it is expected that changes will follow on both sides of the fence.

Apart from the moments of national importance in World Cup and Tests there has been much to cheer all around the country. Perhaps we should have anticipated something out of the ordinary from the moment Alec Bedser, Chairman of the England Selectors, holed in one at Stoke Poges golf course. He was in receipt of a stroke at that hole and playing Stableford rules gained 6 points. Not bad for a five iron tee shot!

Derbyshire's Bob Taylor set up a new John Player record for wicket-keeping when he took six catches and made one stumping in Derbyshire's match at Old Trafford.

Gloucestershire's 62 against Hampshire was the lowest score ever in the Benson and Hedges competition. The Australian Alan Turner scored a hundred (151) on his debut in England. Colin Cowdrey did decide to retire and not to be tempted to play cricket for Sussex. Geoff

Boycott was the first batsman to reach 1,000 runs this season. It was during Yorkshire's match against Somerset on June 28th.

Keith Boyce of Essex scored a century in only 58 minutes against Leicestershire at Chelmsford. It was the fastest hundred since Joe Hardstaff's in 51 minutes for Notts against Kent in 1937. He was soon overtaken however in the most unlikely way by his teammate Robin Hobbs who thrashed a century against Australia at Chelmsford on August 26th in 44 minutes. It is the fifth fastest century ever recorded and was taken off 45 balls, including seven sixes and twelve fours.

Gordon Greenidge of Hampshire scored a magnificent 259 against Sussex at Southampton, the season's highest individual score. His 13 sixes that day surpassed C. J. Barnett's record of 11 for Gloucestershire against Somerset in 1934.

Hampshire established a new limited-over innings record in the second round of the Gillette Cup against Glamorgan. 371 for 4 was the team record and Greenidge beat his own individual score record for one-day cricket with 177.

Malcolm Nash of Glamorgan, on the wrong side that time, certainly reminded Hampshire of his talents with the new ball at Basingstoke in the Championship match. He took 9 for 56 in the first innings and 14 for 137 in the match. F. W. Swarbrook took 9 wickets for 20 against Sussex at Hove—the best bowling performance of the season.

Poor Mike Proctor tried hard to come back into Gloucestershire's side after operations on his knee. He bowled off-spinners for a while but in the Gillette Cup match at Old Trafford against Lancashire he twisted the knee badly, left the field, and did not play out the end of the season.

Geoff Boycott and John Hampshire set a new John Player record for any wicket by scoring 186 for the first wicket against Gloucestershire at Scarborough. However it was a year when Gloucestershire secured their future with the help of the Phoenix Assurance Company who purchased the County ground at Bristol for £125,000. They will spend another £100,000 to develop it and lease it back to Gloucestershire for 99 years.

Perhaps I should end at the level where the game is played with equal effort and love, but not for money, and that is with the villages. From Gowerton in South Wales came hundreds of supporters to Lord's to cheer their team for the second year in succession at Lord's. Last time they lost, this time they were too good for Isleham. There was nothing rustic about the cricket. The game is obviously strong in these later stages of the competition but the sight of an informal massed choir taking over the cocktail party after the game was a little unusual to say the least.

I have never heard the sacred rafters at Lord's ring with the sounds of Cwm Rhondda. When the Welsh win there is no danger of us being quiet about it.

So whether one's lasting impression was of Greig's fightback, Steele's grey hair and jockey cap going out to meet Lillee and Thomson, or one of the other marvellous moments of this sunny season, there was inspiration for everyone, certainly enough to send young boys racing to the nets, and that cannot be bad, can it?